e-Learning Skills

Alan Clarke

First published 2004 by
PALGRAVE MACMILLAN
Houndmills, Basingstoke, Hampshire RG21 6XS and
175 Fifth Avenue, New York, N.Y. 10010
Companies and representatives throughout the world

PALGRAVE MACMILLAN is the global academic imprint of the Palgrave Macmillan division of St. Martin's Press, LLC and of Palgrave Macmillan Ltd. Macmillan® is a registered trademark in the United States, United Kingdom and other countries. Palgrave is a registered trademark in the European Union and other countries.

ISBN-13: 978–4039–1755–3
ISBN-10: 1–4039–1755–8

This book is printed on paper suitable for recycling and made from fully managed and sustained forest sources.

A catalogue record for this book is available from the British Library.

10 9 8 7 6 5 4 3 2
13 12 11 10 09 08 07 06 05

Printed and bound in China

Contents

Acknowledgements

I would like to thank my wife Christine for her help and support throughout an extremely busy period of our lives during which this book was written.

The author and publishers wish to acknowledge Google, Microsoft Corporation and Sheffield College for the use of screen capture images.

Screen shots reprinted by permission from Microsoft Corporation. Microsoft Windows, Office, Word, Excel, PowerPoint, Access, Internet Explorer, Outlook, Paint, MSN and Windows Explorer are the registered trademarks of the Microsoft Corporation. All other trademarks are the property of their respective owners.

Introduction

The term 'e-learning' covers a wide range of techniques and methods. It includes the use of technology as part of a conventional or traditional course as well as an online course where learners and tutors will never meet face-to-face. This wide spectrum of applications makes confusion a real possibility. Throughout this book, the term 'e-learning' will be used to include the whole range, but the emphasis will be on the use of technology to open up wider opportunities for learners, such as learning at a distance by using communication technologies. The book should be suitable for those who are learning at a distance or at a college that has integrated e-learning into its programmes. The term 'college' has been used throughout, but e-learning is provided by many different organisations such as universities, private e-learning companies, employers and many other organisations. Please assume 'college' is a generic term covering all locations.

Within the book is a range of activities. To gain the most value, you should attempt as many of them as possible. Many are followed by a section entitled 'discussion' that provides some general feedback on the task. This should only be considered once you have undertaken the activity.

There are many references to websites throughout the book. However, the world wide web is a dynamic environment with sites continuously developing, changing and in some cases disappearing. If you cannot locate a site directly through its address (URL), then use keywords from the text and search the world wide web to locate it or similar sites.

There are many ways to use the contents of the book to aid the development of your learning skills. You can simply work through the chapters in sequence, or you can try to identify your needs and concentrate on developing particular skills and knowledge. Appendix A ('Assessing your Learning Skills') provides you with a checklist and a cross reference to the chapters which contain information and activities to address relevant skill areas. Appendix C ('Assessing your ICT

Skills') serves a similar purpose with regard to your computer skills. It provides a checklist which allows you to assess your needs. Chapter 3 is designed to help you develop some computer skills that are appropriate to learning, such as presenting information, copyright and plagiarism. If you already are a skilled computer user, then you can probably skip this chapter.

Each chapter is designed to offer you a different insight into e-learning:

- Chapter 1 aims to offer you an introduction to e-learning, how it is different from traditional methods and what you can expect from it.
- Chapter 2 aims to refresh your awareness of traditional learning skills: e-learning skills are built upon a foundation of traditional skills.
- Chapter 3 aims to provide you with an introduction to information and communication technology skills particularly relevant to e-learning (e.g. searching the world wide web for information).
- Chapter 4 aims to introduce you to the learning environments and approaches that you will encounter as an e-learner.
- Chapter 5 aims to explore the nature of e-learning skills with you.
- Chapter 6 provides you with additional practice to help you develop e-learning skills.
- Chapter 7 is designed to help you consider the nature of communication technologies that can help you take part in e-learning courses and programmes.
- Chapter 8 assists you in considering the nature of working and learning with others as part of an e-learning course (i.e. collaborative and co-operative learning).
- Chapter 9 provides you with a range of online resources.

The Contents list gives you the titles of each section and the index should help you locate particular topics.

1 What is e-Learning?

▶ Introduction

All parts of the education and training system are enthusiastically exploring and implementing e-learning in one form or another. In many ways, a revolution is underway and many people have made a comparison with the impact on learning of printing and the mass production of books. While this is an appropriate comparison, there are numerous differences, not least the timescale of the developments. e-Learning has exploded on the awareness of education and training professionals and widespread use has been achieved in a few years, whereas printing took centuries to reach large numbers of people. The pace of change is accelerating and new approaches are being tried almost every day. e-Learning is a major force for change.

'e-Learning' is a general term covering many different approaches that have in common the use of information and communication technologies. Terms and concepts are very new and often different language and jargon is used to describe similar approaches. This can make it difficult to understand what is involved in the learning programme. In this book we are concentrating on the use of e-learning to free learners from a rigid timetable of attendance at a college or other learning institution. This includes the delivery of learning at a distance from a tutor or institution, but it can also add a degree of freedom to more traditional programmes, for example allowing online discussion groups to accompany a lecture programme, delivering a programme based on interactive multimedia learning materials in a college learning centre and a distance learning programme with learners based across a whole country.

Some common terms which you may encounter are:

- online learning;
- computer-based learning;
- blended learning;

1

- learning objects;
- learning resources;
- distributed learning;
- interactive learning materials;
- computer mediated learning;
- computer mediated communication;
- web-based training.

Universal definitions of these widely used terms have not been agreed. It is good practice to ask users of the terms to explain what they mean by them. Online and e-learning, for example, are sometimes used interchangeably, while on other occasions they are seen as being different. The glossary at the end of the book provides explanations of many terms that you may come into contact with.

'e-Learning' and 'online learning' are general terms covering a wide range of approaches. They may combine a mixture of different elements such as:

- information and communication technology;
- interaction;
- learning resources;
- collaborative and individual learning;
- formal and informal learning;
- support.

There is considerable variation in the way the components are integrated together. e-Learning can simply consist of visiting websites to locate material that can help you complete an assignment. The websites may have been specially produced as part of the education or training programme or may have been designed for a wider purpose. In many ways, this is similar to asking you to visit the library to locate books and other materials. The teacher may provide you with a booklist or a list of websites or simply a list of topics. In both cases you need the skills to locate the material, whether they be searching a library or the world wide web. There are both things in common and distinct differences within the search skills involved in traditional and e-learning.

► Comparison of traditional and e-learning skills

Table 1.1 shows a straightforward comparison of traditional and e-learning skills. Many of the individual skills can be broken down into a variety of sub- or related skills.

For example:

Reading skills   browsing/scanning skills (particularly important when using the world wide web to locate relevant websites)

Writing   summarising the key points
referencing information
keeping records

Research skills searching skills are essentially a part of research skills

The table is not intended to cover all the sub-skills, but merely to provide an initial basis for comparison.

The two major differences between traditional and e-learning skills are the context and degree of importance of the skill. e-Learners may be learning at a distance from both their peers and tutors, so they need to be far more self-sustained than the traditional learner. Traditional learning provides many informal opportunities, such as a brief chat in the corridor with other learners, to discover their views, whereas e-learning requires you to send an email, a more formal activity. Learners have had years of practice in face-to-face communicating but most will be relatively inexperienced at being dependent on short written messages (i.e. email or chat).

In face-to-face communications you can see the facial expressions of people, hear the tone of voice and listen to the words used. In e-learning you only have the written words to communicate through and this notoriously leads to misunderstandings. It is more difficult to convey precise meaning. Various ways have been developed to help convey emotions such as the use of emoticons, a code based on punctuation or other symbols such as:

- ☺   happy
- ☹   sad
- using capitals or uppercase means you are shouting.

However, only a minority of email users include emoticons and they are inevitably basic in comparison to the non-verbal communication that everyone has grown up using. They may be confusing if the person receiving the message does not understand their purpose.

Table 1.1   Comparing learning skills

Traditional skills	e-Learning skills	Difference
Time management	Time management	Time management is critical in e-learning since it provides greater opportunity to take control of your own learning. This is also true of other forms of open and distance learning.
Acceptance of responsibility	Acceptance of responsibility	e-Learning provides more opportunities for learners to take responsibility for their learning than traditional learning does. This is also true of other forms of open and distance learning.
Planning	Planning	The benefits of e-learning include giving learners more freedom to choose when and how they study, so placing on them the emphasis for planning. Traditional courses are often determined by the tutor and are accompanied by timetables and study guides. This is also true of other forms of open and distance learning.
Searching skills – libraries	Searching skills – world wide web	Scale – the world wide web is enormous in comparison to any physical library.
Assessing quality – written and other physical content	Assessing quality – world wide web	The world wide web has few quality assurance mechanisms. Books and other printed educational content have established means of judging quality. Anyone can launch a website, but producing a textbook requires the agreement of publishers, peers and reviewers.
Listening – to peers and teachers during presentations and discussions	Listening is required only occasionally e.g. when the programme is based on audio or video conferencing	Listening is a key skill in most forms of traditional learning, while it is frequently only plays a minority role or none at all in e-learning.

→

Table 1.1   Comparing learning skills – *continued*

Traditional skills	e-Learning skills	Difference
Reading – mainly printed material	Reading is a key skill in e-learning. Most information is presented as text displayed on a screen.	Since a majority of the material is text, reading is a key skill in e-learning comparable to the roles reading *and* listening play in traditional learning
		Browsing is the normal way that the content of websites is read to locate relevant content.
Writing – mostly in the form of note taking or completing exercises (e.g. essays)	Writing (keyboard skills) – for communications, note taking and exercises	Writing (keyboard skills) is essential for e-learning communication (e.g. email) as well as for note taking and exercises. Writing is the main online communication method.
Self-assessment	Self-assessment	This is a key skill in all forms of learning. In traditional learning there are many opportunities to compare your performance with your peers (e.g. observing them in class, sharing results in the coffee lounge, etc.). In e-learning their performance is often invisible to you.
		You need to find new ways of assessing your own performance.
Collaborating with others face-to-face	Collaborating with others through communication software (e.g. email)	The key difference is time. A face-to-face group will often agree regular meetings so that tasks are achieved quickly. Online group members will each have their own time scales and may well live in different time zones, so that collaboration is often spread over a long period. Motivation is sometimes difficult to maintain.
Problem solving – individually or small groups	Problem solving – individually or with a group at a distance	The significant difference when working with others is that in e-learning they are at a distance and it is therefore difficult to judge their views.

Traditional learners have the benefit of a tutor's judgement in observing their group and realising that some individuals are confused by the topic or that others need to be reminded about a forthcoming test. An e-learning tutor has far less information on which to base a judgement, so the e-learner needs to be more self-reliant. Time management skills become more important since you need to be in control of your learning. You cannot rely on a tutor or peers informally reminding you of deadlines. In later chapters you will be given the opportunity to develop these skills.

e-Learning assumes you are a competent and confident user of computers and communication technology. In Chapter 3 you will be provided with help to improve or revise your technological skills.

▶ What makes a successful e-learner?

e-Learning is a new development, which means that there is not a lot of good evidence yet of what makes a successful e-learner. However, some characteristics are:

* confidence as an independent, successful learner, especially when learning in non-formal settings (e.g. in your home, work or community);
* a positive attitude to learning;
* being self-motivated to succeed;
* having effective communication skills;
* an ability to collaborate and co-operate with other learners;
* being a competent and confident user of ICT.

(See Nipper 1989; Clarke 1998; Palloff and Pratt 1999; Clarke 2002a.)

▶ Benefits of e-learning

Your main benefits as an e-learner are that you have considerable freedom of choice over:

* place;
* pace;
* time.

Activity   Assessment of skills

It is useful to start any learning process by assessing your starting point, so consider the lists of traditional and e-learning skills and judge your own competence in each one. In a later chapter you will consider your computer and communication technology skills.

Traditional skills	Competence			e-Learning skills	Competence		
	Poor	*Acceptable*	*Excellent*		*Poor*	*Acceptable*	*Excellent*
Searching skills – libraries				Searching skills – world wide web			
Assessing quality – written and other physical content				Assessing quality – world wide web			
Listening				Listening			
Reading				Reading			
Writing				Writing			
Self-assessment				Self-assessment			
Collaborating with others face-to-face				Collaborating with others at a distance			
Problem-solving				Problem-solving			
Time management				Time management			
Acceptance of responsibility				Acceptance of responsibility			
Planning				Planning			

Discussion

If your experience of e-learning is limited, you may find that you have marked yourself low against the various characteristics. However, many traditional learning skills are very useful in online settings. You just need to be able to transfer and adjust them to the new context. This may appear a difficult process at the moment but with the help of the content and activities within this book you will achieve this skill.

Appendix A provides another checklist to help you consider your e-learning skills. It is cross-referenced to the various parts of this book to allow you to identify sections that will help you develop particular skills.

Activity Successful learner

Consider your own experience of learning and decide how successful a learner
you are. You should consider all types of learning, especially your ability to learn
independently (e.g. teach yourself to repair a washing machine, to understand
instructions or plan a holiday) as well as more formal studies:

1. Are you confident that you can learn new ideas, concepts and skills in a variety
    of learning environments (e.g. teaching yourself)?
2. Do you enjoy learning new things and normally finish what you start?
3. Do you work well with other learners?

Write some brief notes

Discussion

If you have been a successful learner, then it is likely that you will continue to be
successful in online courses. This is not simply about your success on formal
education courses, but in the wider sense of learning independently (e.g. teaching
yourself skills and knowledge in any context).

Online courses are different from traditional forms of learning, so if you have had
little previous success in learning this is an opportunity to make a new start. If you
have had problems in traditional courses with restrictive timetables, travelling
arrangements or the pace of the course, then e-learning may help you overcome
them.

1. **Are you confident that you can learn new ideas, concepts and skills?**
    E-learning tends to ask learners to take more responsibility for their own
    learning than traditional approaches. If you feel that you need a lot of support,
    guidance and direction from tutors, then you should check if the course is right
    for you or work towards developing the skills that you will need. Many colleges
    offer support to develop study skills.

2. **Do you enjoy learning new things and normally finish what you start?**
    e-Learning uses many different methods and technologies, so it favours
    learners who enjoy new challenges and ideas. Does taking on new challenges
    motivate you?

3. **Do you work well with other learners?**
    Although e-learning tends to be discussed as if it is about individualised
    learning, many methods include group, collaborative and co-operative learning.
    These require people who can build relationships with other learners.

Appendix B contains a list of tips for the successful e-learner and you may want to
consider it alongside this feedback.

You are potentially free to study at any location you want. So if you like to work at home, you can combine studying with family responsibilities or avoid the frustrations of commuting.

The tutor and other learners in the class or group often set the pace of studying. e-Learning gives you the choice of how quickly or slowly to learn. If you want to work through the night, you can or if you like to fit short bursts of activity into your timetable to allow for taking care of elderly parents or children, you are free to do so.

All traditional courses have a fixed timetable of classes and activities around which you must work. e-Learning provides you with a considerable degree of choice. You can study in the middle of the night or during the day, whatever is best for you.

► Learning styles

Everyone has preferred ways of learning and these are sometimes referred to as learning styles. When you have to learn in a manner that is different from your preferred learning style, you will often feel

---

Activity   e-learning

In choosing to be an e-learner you need to question your assumptions about the suitability of the approaches. Consider the questions below:

- What benefits are you seeking from the e-learning programme?
- What do you hope to achieve from becoming an e-learner?
- Are your objectives realistic?
- Could you achieve your objectives through a traditional course?

Write some brief notes about these questions.

Discussion

There are various motives for selecting an e-learning course rather than a traditional one. You may want to combine your studies with a job or family responsibilities and an e-learning course will give you the flexibility you need. You may have been attracted by these new approaches to studying. Regardless of your reasons, you will still need to work just as hard as on a traditional course. However, you have more choice of when, where and at what pace to learn. This places a lot of responsibility on you that in a traditional course is provided by its structure and the tutor.

The structure of e-learning courses varies considerably, so you need to ensure that the selected course will meet your expectations.

uncomfortable and perhaps express doubts about the suitability of the approach. However, you have probably had experience of a wide range of learning styles during your education and successfully coped with them, but this does not mean that you prefer them or seek them out. Some you will probably avoid because your own experience has shown you that you are uncomfortable with them and struggle to learn with them.

There are a variety of ways of expressing learning styles, but one which is appropriate to e-learning considers preferences in terms of the seeing, hearing and doing. If you are a learner who prefers visual learning (i.e. seeing) then you will like:

- learning materials that include plenty of pictures, graphics, video and animation;
- images that support text.

If you are a learner who prefers auditory learning (i.e. listening) then you will favour:

- discussing ideas with other students (e.g. mailgroups, bulletin boards, chatrooms and email);
- group working (e.g. groupware and collaborative/co-operative working);
- sound effects;
- video clips.

If you are a learner who prefers kinaesthetic learning (i.e. doing) then you will opt for:

- activities (e.g. lots of action – making choices);
- making notes;
- taking part in group work.

Some of these preferences translate straightforwardly into the e-learning environment. e-Learning is generally strong in providing many opportunities to make choices, to interact with content with a large visual element and to work with others through communication technologies.

There are other ways of considering preferences (Kolb, 1984; Honey and Munford, 1986) than in terms of the visual, auditory and kinaesthetic. You could consider your preferences in relation to the following characteristics:

Activity   Learning preferences

Consider your own experience of learning and try to recall what you liked and disliked about the learning approaches. Try to write a list of what you enjoyed, disliked, etc.

Discussion

Personally, I like to learn by doing most of the time but I also enjoy trying to analyse new material comparing and contrasting it with existing knowledge. In order to reflect on new experiences I need to go for a walk. I find it difficult to reflect simply sitting in a chair or reading a book. I need some form of activity. I probably prefer visual content and I am comfortable learning on my own.

There is no reason why your own analysis should resemble mine. The key point is to be aware of your own preferences so that you can take account of them when you are learning. If you need to take a walk in order to reflect, then build that walk into your study timetable.

Consider the nature of the e-learning course you are intending to take part in and decide if it supports your learning preferences.

- **reflection** – you may like to have time to reflect on experiences, learning content and discussion;
- **analytical** – you may prefer to analyse new content, ideas systematically, etc.;
- **holistic** – you like to know the overall picture and are uncomfortable having the subject built up slowly, which is often the approach taken in lectures or presentations. You will appreciate overviews, abstracts and summaries.

Preferences are not mutually exclusive. Most people have a mix of them. If you consider your own experience of learning, you will be able to identify what you like and dislike about the learning approaches you have experienced. It is important for you to be aware of your own preferences and the nature of e-learning.

▶ Information and communication technology

e-Learning is learning through and being supported by the use of information technology. It therefore assumes that you are able to exploit technology. Most education and training providers will offer a technical helpline so that if you are studying at home or at a distance you can gain assistance. However, helplines do assume you have sufficient understanding of the technology to follow their instructions.

You are free to study at many different locations, including learning centres provided by colleges, companies, internet cafes and community sites. Often they will charge for the time spent online. However, they do provide assistance if you have technical problems, thus removing some of the stress. If you are studying using a college's own resources, then many of the technical issues will be handled by them.

Computers are powerful aids to your learning and can help you by providing:

- ways to organise and store your notes, references and materials (e.g. folders, files and databases);
- tools to present your work (e.g. word processing, presentation graphics, charts and graphs);
- tools to analyse your data (e.g. spreadsheets);
- equipment to capture evidence (e.g. digital cameras and scanners);
- access to the enormous library of information that the world wide web represents.

These aids are not confined to e-learning, but are useful ways of assisting your studies in traditional, blended or e-learning courses. Many learners undertake traditional and e-learning modules at the same time.

▶ Interaction

When you speak to a tutor or another learner you expect them to respond to your words and in return you will react to them. The e-learning equivalent of this dialogue is called interactivity and it is achieved, of course, through email, chat, bulletin boards and other forms of communication. Good learning materials and environments should respond to your actions in appropriate and helpful ways to engage you and, hopefully, assist you to learn.

Interactivity can be very simple. In some applications a small label will appear to help you understand an icon when you place your mouse pointer on top of that icon. The system is responding to your action.

It is useful to consider interaction as a dialogue between yourself and the learning system through what appears on the screen and the input devices (e.g. mouse and keyboard). This is called the interface. Figure 1.1 shows this model of interaction. Any learning system should offer you a considerable degree of support, many opportunities for helpful

Two-way dialogue

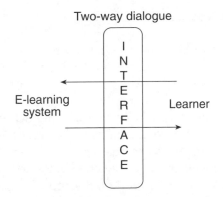

Figure 1.1   Simple communication between a learner and e-learning content

dialogue and provide you with lots of choice. In a sense, it is adapting to your needs similarly to the way that tutors will adjust their approach to meet your requirements. To take advantage of these possibilities, you need to explore the interface. It is therefore good practice to systematically investigate the interface when you first encounter the system. You will frequently be offered an introduction to the system or a guided tour of the facilities. If this is not automatically suggested to you, then seek it out. It is often included in the help system, the introduction or on the home page.

Many learning systems offer a virtual learning centre with what appears to be traditional equipment such as desks, computers, flipcharts, coffee bars and books. There is often the intention that these resources will behave in similar ways to the actual objects and facilities. That is:

- a coffee bar (or common room, refectory, etc.) provides the means to communicate with other learners through an electronic chatroom or similar facility;
- desks may provide the links to the administration;
- books and floppy disks are like handouts and other support;
- computers refer to computer applications such as email.

Virtual environments vary considerably in appearance and structure, so you need to explore them to ensure you can take advantage of the resources. This is the equivalent of physically walking around a college campus on your first day to discover where everything is located. It is a vital step in your preparation for the course.

► Learning resources

Learning resources often play a significant role in e-learning. The materials may take a variety of forms depending on the course and approach taken. They include:

*   Interactive materials that you access and interact with online. The materials can cover the whole subject or merely some aspects, but are designed to enhance learning
*   Standalone interactive materials such as multimedia CD-ROMs.
*   Traditional materials (e.g. workbooks, open learning texts and lecture notes) which are made available to you online, through the post or in the college library.
*   Resources which are simply available on the world wide web (e.g. webpages, downloadable files and online databases). Chapter 9 provides an extensive list of resources on the world wide web that support e-learning skills development.

Your e-learning course may have some or none of these forms of learning material, depending on the subject and approach being taken. The key issue for you is that you need to be able to learn no matter how the course is designed. This requires that you are able to use interactive and other learning materials, analyse written content and locate and assess web-based content. These skills will be considered in later chapters.

► Collaborative and individual learning

Face-to-face and e-learning can involve both group and individual activities. It is also perfectly possible to have a course involving both e-learning and traditional methods. It is widely accepted that online groups are often more effective if they are initially formed by some type of face-to-face meetings. However, it is not always possible to bring everyone together if they are living across a country or on several continents. A significant benefit of online learning is that it allows people to participate who cannot physically attend a particular educational institute. It allows learners from many different cultures to learn together and benefit from each other's experiences. Online learners are individuals who can collaborate with their peers through communication technology. This use of technology to allow people to communicate is sometimes called computer mediated communication (CMC).

Activity   Learning materials – 1

During your education you will have come into contact with many types of learning materials. Consider how you have used them and what you found useful in the different kinds. Record your impressions of the different types.

Discussion

Some types of learning materials I have encountered are:

- **Handouts** – they are useful since they save note taking, but I have found that it is best to have them before the lecture or presentation so I can annotate them with extra thoughts while I am listening.
- **Webpages** – the world wide web seems to have information about almost everything I need to know about, so is very useful. However, you do have to wade through a lot of materials sometimes to find what you want.
- **Study guides** – I have always found a complete overview to the course and suggestions on how to study extremely useful.

There are many other forms of learning materials that you may have mentioned including videos, open learning packs, self-tests, text books and case studies.

Activity   Learning materials – 2

Interactive materials are an important part of some e-learning programmes and it is important that you have some experience of them. In many college, company and community learning centres you can gain access to interactive learning materials. The learning centre staff will be able to help you to use the material, if you have never used that type before. Work your way through a package and record your first impressions. If you already have experience of interactive content, then reflect on what you did and record your impression.

Discussion

Interactive learning packages should engage you and provide you with a motivating and interesting experience of the subject being studied. You should have considerable freedom to explore the materials, to retrace your steps and have another go at exercises. You should be able to stop and mark your place so that you can return to and start from where you finished. The presentation of content should be to a high standard.

Unfortunately, not all interactive packages meet this standard. The cost of developing professional interactive materials is very high, so that some packages are little more than an electronic book. You should ask yourself if a paper book would have served the same or a more effective purpose.

▶ Formal and informal learning

e-Learning courses involve both formal and informal learning. The world wide web is an enormous learning resource, available to any learner. However, in order to take advantage of it, users require the skills of searching, identifying and evaluating content. This is sometimes called information literacy. This indicates the balance of e-learning in that the potential is huge but the skills required to benefit from it successfully are significant. Informal learning is frequently incorporated into conventional and more formal e-learning courses.

Many organisations are developing formal e-learning courses, but experience is relatively limited so that ideas and approaches are essentially still being explored. However, in order to benefit from the flexibility of online approaches, formal learning needs to include the freedom to learn when, where and at what pace the learner chooses. More formal courses have:

- a start and finish date (i.e. complete freedom is reduced but is still substantial);
- assessment standards (e.g. a traditional examination on completion);
- intermediate deadlines (e.g. reports required by set dates).

Learners are more likely to drop out when too much responsibility is thrust on them too quickly. A degree of structure is often helpful and devices such as intermediate reports can help identify learners who need assistance. Some courses provide trial assignments to allow practice in writing assignments. It is often difficult to judge when to offer help in a completely open-ended course.

▶ Support

All forms of distance learning, including e-learning, suffer from higher levels of dropout than conventional face-to-face courses. The key to successful distance learning is the degree of support that is available to you. Support is not limited to the formal support of your tutors but can include:

- other learners;
- study circles/groups;

Activity   Support

What sort of support do you need when you are studying? Do you want to be in control of your own learning or do you need someone to directly motivate, encourage and remind you of the course deadlines. Write some brief notes and reflect on the nature of e-learning, especially if you are learning at a distance.

Discussion

Personally, I like to feel in control of my own learning, so I am content to plan my own studies and to take responsibility for meeting deadlines. However, I have always enjoyed the support of my family who have encouraged and motivated me to study. In terms of more formal support, I have always found it useful to know that there is someone to telephone or email to ask for advice. In several courses, I have developed contacts with other learners so that we can swap ideas and answer each other's questions.

- family;
- friends;
- learning centre staff;
- workplace instructors;
- mentors;
- tutors.

A supportive family can be the difference between success and failure. When you are choosing to take part in an e-learning course you should consider what support is available to you both formally (e.g. tutors, mentors and other learners) and informally (e.g. friends and family). Is the course structured to encourage mutual support between the learners? Is a mentor provided and is a personal tutor appointed for you? These are important questions to ask before starting the course.

▶ Tutor's role

There are significant differences between a traditional and an e-learning tutor. Table 1.2 compares the traditional and e-learning roles. e-Learning is often presented as learner-centred, while traditional education and training is seen as tutor-centred. The e-learner is given control and allowed to make the significant choices of what, when and how to study the material. In traditional learning, the tutor is essentially in command of the process. These are both stereotypes and the

Table 1.2 Comparison of tutor roles

Activity	Traditional	e-Learning
Lecture	Tutor is the presenter of information and decides what to communicate, the sequence of information and the speed of delivery.	Information is often presented as learning material so the tutor's role is to facilitate and assist the learner to understand. The learner chooses the pace, content and sequence of learning.
		Tutors will react to learners' requests although some will offer proactive help based on their experience.
Individual assignments	The norm in many forms of traditional teaching is for the tutor to set individual assignments. They are an important part of the assessment process.	Individual assignments are employed for similar purposes as in traditional methods.
		They are also used to assist learners to self assess and are often designed centrally rather than by the individual tutor.
Group assignments	These are relatively rare in many forms of traditional learning. Group assignments are frequently used and devised by tutors within courses to explore ideas rather than as assessments.	e-Learning also uses group assignments which serve a similar purpose to traditional courses.
	Tutors will facilitate the groups.	One of the main differences is that assignments are more often used for assessment in e-learning and are sometimes designed centrally rather than by the tutor.
		Co-operative and collaborative learning approaches are employed in e-learning. ➜

design of all types of courses and approaches varies considerably. Just by presenting a course online will not in itself ensure it is learner-centred. Many traditional courses do offer a considerable degree of choice to the learner. The comparison does assume the stereotype to aid the discussion, but it is important to realise that it depends on the design of the programme. You should ask about the design of your programme and the underpinning intentions before starting it and then consider whether it meets your needs.

Table 1.2 Comparison of tutor roles – *continued*

Activity	Traditional	e-Learning
Feedback	Feedback uses a mixture of methods but verbal face-to-face is frequently the dominant one.	Feedback again employs a range of methods, but written feedback is often important where learning is taking place at a distance from the tutor.
Assessment	The tutor is often also the examiner, devising the assessment and marking the answers.	e-Learning often contains many tests or assessments for the student to undertake and are then marked by the software. These are intended to help learners to self-assess.
Support	Formal support is frequently provided face-to-face by a variety of people including tutors, mentors and other support staff.

Peers, friends and family sometimes offer informal support. | Support is probably more important, as the risk of isolation is greater if you are studying at a distance. The tutor and other formal support workers may be less visible due to the distance and their role is more facilitation than direct delivery of learning.

Peer support is important in e-learning and often the course will be structured to encourage this. |

In most traditional learning environments (e.g. college and training centre), the tutor is probably the most important component in the students' learning experience. Tutors provide the critical elements of:

- **Support** – help when things go wrong or to prevent errors.
- **Direction** – showing the key issues in understanding the subject.
- **Explanation** – feedback on progression and advice on what is good practice.
- **Content** – presenting content in a way that can be readily understood.
- **Responsibility** – tutors accept some of the responsibility for learning (e.g. sending reminders about deadlines).
- **Structure** – they design and manage the structure of the course.

The role of the tutor's role in e-learning courses is different. They are facilitators and moderators of your learning rather than directors or managers as in conventional learning situations. This places more responsibility for your learning on yourself in e-learning, but it does not mean that your tutor is not a critical resource. A tutor can provide you with a great deal of help. The nature of online learning is such that it is difficult for your tutor to immediately identify if you have a problem. They will be monitoring your behaviour by considering how often you send messages to the course conference, as well as their content. However, emails tend to be short and focused, so that diagnosing problems is more difficult than in face-to-face situations. If you are unsure or puzzled you need to ask your tutor for help directly.

The online tutor provides the key elements of:

- **Welcome/confidence** – helping you to feel comfortable in the online environment (e.g. by encouraging you to take part in online conferences).
- **Support** – through answering questions, making suggestions and moderating discussion so that you do not exceed the agreed standards.
- **Feedback** – annotating assignments, posting messages, etc.
- **Facilitation** – encouraging discussion and participation so that a climate of mutual support is created.
- **Monitoring** – considering the activities of each learner so that problems are identified as soon as possible.

There are some significant differences between the tutor's role in traditional and e-learning courses. One way of describing the difference is that traditional courses are tutor-centred, while e-learning is more learner-centred. This is relative, since a great deal depends on how the online course is designed.

► How to assess an e-learning course/programme

A key aspect of any form of learning is to choose the right course for yourself. This section aims to help you assess possible e-learning courses or programmes by providing you with a checklist. The list is in no particular order, since e-learning courses can take many different forms and place the emphasis in variety of ways. Some of the items will require you to study later parts of this book so, at the moment, they will not be clear, but it is useful to attempt to use the checklist to assess courses now and then update it as you work through the book.

You should also check on other aspects of the course (e.g. qualifications, the standing of the college or provider, and value for money). To assess the e-learning aspects, you should systematically ask about these topics. Some of the information should be available from the college or provider's website and their publications. However, you may need to ask additional questions.

The decision about the course is yours to make and e-learning is a mix of different features and services, so many combinations are likely to be effective. However, you may well have expectations that are best confirmed at the start.

1.   **Content** – how is the content provided?

     * specifically designed material for the course;
     * interactive content which meets a published standard;
     * traditional materials (e.g. books and other printed content) which is integrated with high quality support and communication technology.

2.   **Methods** – what teaching and learning methods are employed?

     * e-learning is blended/integrated with traditional methods;
     * distance learning;
     * any face-to-face contact with peers and tutors;
     * degree of freedom (i.e. choice of place, pace and time).

3.   **Feedback** – how is feedback provided?

     * annotation of assignments;
     * personal tutor/mentor;
     * learners conference and/or chatroom;
     * is there a standard for replying to your messages (e.g. 24 hours).

4.   **Learning environment** – what online environments are provided?

     * virtual learning environment;
     * managed learning environment;
     * intranet/extranet;
     * website.

5. **Support** – what support is provided?

    -   individual tutor/mentor;
    -   links/communication with other learners.

6. **Assessment** – how is the course assessed?

    -   online assessment;
    -   conventional assessment (e.g. written examination);
    -   continuous assessment;
    -   peer assessment.

7. **Flexibility** – how much choice does the course provide?

    -   freedom to choose place, pace and time;
    -   fixed timetable.

8. **Standards** – does the organisation provide a statement of its e-learning standards (e.g. minimum requirements for content)?

If you are considering a course, then apply the checklist and it should help you make a more systematic assessment.

▶ Summary

1. **What is e-learning?**
    e-Learning is a general term covering many different learning approaches that have in common the use of information and communication technologies.

2. **Comparison – traditional and e-learning skills**
    There are many things common to the learning skills required for traditional and e-learning courses, but the main differences are:

    -   e-learners are learning at a distance from both their peers and tutors;
    -   e-learning is more formal with less opportunity for informal communication (e.g. chat in the corridor);
    -   e-learners often have relatively little experience of email and other communication technologies compared to face-to-face;

face-to-face is an immediate communication method while e-learning often involves a delay;

- e-learning depends on written communication which makes it difficult to convey emotion;
- e-learners need to be more independent and self-reliant than traditional learners.

3.   What makes a successful e-learner?

The characteristics of a successful e-learner are self-confidence, motivation, a positive attitude, being a good communicator and collaborator and a competent user of ICT.

4.   Benefits of e-learning

e-Learning gives you potentially more freedom to choose the place, pace and time of your learning. However, it does place more responsibility for your learning on you and the design of e-learning courses varies, so the degree of freedom will change from course to course.

5.   Learning styles

All learners have preferences about the way they like to learn. These preferences are called learning styles. There are several ways of describing learning styles, but one that is appropriate to e-learning is in terms of the seeing, hearing and doing. e-Learning provides many opportunities to make choices, interact with content with a large visual element and to work with others through communication technologies.

6.   Information and communication technology

e-Learning is about learning through and being supported by the use of information technology. Learners need to be competent and confident users of ICT.

7.   Interaction

Interaction can be considered as a dialogue between yourself and the learning system through what appears on the screen and the input devices (e.g. mouse and keyboard). Interactive learning materials should engage and motivate you through their ability to adapt to your individual needs.

8. Learning resources

In many forms of e-learning, learning materials play a significant role. Materials can take many different forms including online and standalone interactive materials, workbooks, open learning texts, lecture notes, webpages, downloadable files and online databases.

9. Collaborative and individual learning

e-Learning allows the participation in learning of people who would normally be unable to take part. It provides opportunities to collaborate with learners from many different cultures and backgrounds.

10. Formal and informal learning

The design of e-learning courses varies considerably, so the degree of freedom offered to learners will vary. The flexibility of the programme will depend on the objectives of the course and different courses will have a very different balance of methods and content.

11. Support

Successful e-learners need to be formally and informally supported by tutors, peers, other staff, friends and family.

12. Tutors' role

e-Learning should be more learner-centred than traditional education and training, which is often described as tutor-centred. Tutors act more as facilitators and supporters of learners rather than controllers or directors. The responsibility for your learning lies with yourself.

13. How to assess an e-learning course/programme

You should systematically consider what you want from an e-learning course and, using the checklist, assess if it is going to meet your needs.

2 Traditional Skills

To be a successful e-learner you need a foundation of traditional learning skills on which to build your e-learning skills. If you are returning to learning after a significant interval, this chapter will help you to review and revise your skills. If you have well-developed learning skills, it aims to show how your existing skills can be employed in the e-learning environment (i.e. it will assist you to transfer your learning skills to the new situation). The chapter compares traditional and e-learning skills. It considers:

- writing notes;
- reading;
- self-assessment;
- research skills;
- learning in face-to-face groups;
- stress.

▶ Note taking

There are four main reasons for making notes:

1. To record the contents of a lecture, seminar or other learning activity so that you can later use the notes to help you revise or aid your efforts in completing assignments.
2. To help you concentrate during a lecture, seminar or other learning activity. Undertaking an activity such as taking notes during a presentation can assist you to focus on the content, while simply listening is often less effective.
3. To assist you to understand the content of the learning activity, since note taking encourages you to analyse what you are hearing.
4. To convert the content of the learning activity into your own words.

e-Learning does not provide an event at which you are required to take notes. All the content is presented in a form that you could save as an electronic file or print out. It would seem that you have the ultimate in note taking in that you can capture everything. However, the danger is that, since you can save everything, there is no need to read the material or make any particular effort to understand the content. This can lead you into a false sense of security that you have a very comprehensive record of everything and there is no need for you to do anything further. What you actually need to do is read the content and then analyse it. Word processors allow you to annotate electronic text that you have saved or highlight the key phrases using the bold, italic or highlight functions.

It may be that you do not immediately read your notes again. However, this is to miss the opportunity of working from a guide to the content written in your own words. A common problem for many learners is that they are unable to understand their own notes when they come to read them some time later. Good practice is to review your notes soon after you make them to fill in gaps, correct errors and improve on their presentation.

Writing notes

There is a variety of ways of writing notes and a great deal depends on how you like to write. You could write:

- a comprehensive record of the content;
- an outline of the key points;
- a chart or spider diagram of the content;
- the references to other documents, sources and websites.

These ways can all be effective. There are some common points that should be included in all three methods. These are:

- details of the event – title, name of tutor and date;
- aims and objectives of the event;
- how the content relates to other material.

These common features will help you relate your notes to other material when you are reading them again months later. In order to record these features, you do need to concentrate on the start and end of the event when the tutor or facilitator will often introduce and summarise the topics. This will often help you to gain a clear understanding of the content. This is also true of an e-learning experience. The initial email or message will set the scene for the rest of the e-learning event.

You also need to take notes of written content from books, papers or other sources. This is very similar to reading online content (e.g. a website). It is often useful to read with a highlighter pen or a notebook to record the key points. For online content, write down the main issues, since this will help you reflect on the material as well as starting the process of developing a set of notes. You can obviously print or save a webpage but this in itself will not assist your learning. You either need to read the printout, highlight the critical topics, annotate the document or indeed do all of these actions. It is useful to develop your own notes of the content. This can be done using a word processor or paper and pen, depending on your preferences. The key factor is to immerse yourself in the material in order to understand it and relate the content to your existing knowledge.

Group working

Working in small groups is an important approach to learning and is often an integral part of a course. The groups undertake many different tasks (e.g. joint projects, topic discussion, role playing and reviewing material). Note taking is a part of this process but is often difficult to do since group working depends on participation. Combining writing with active involvement is not easy. Usually the notes have to be made later and only a few key points can be recorded during the actual meeting. The quality of the notes depends on your memory and often useful parts of the experience are lost. Group working is frequently a rich learning experience, but this is an important weakness.

Online group working and discussion are broadly similar, except that the whole content of the dialogue can be captured. Many online conferences and mailgroups record every message, so you can review the communication. However, the danger is, once again, simply too much information and it is often useful to produce your own summary. The contents of an online discussion can present you with scores of messages, which is rather like reading a play script without the stage directions. Contributors can send messages whenever they choose, so the order of receipt does not always follow the simple process of a discussion, but may involve backtracking, while in some cases several themes are intertwined with each other.

Activity   Note taking

Read the content below, highlight the key points and annotate the document with your own reflections. Finally, produce your own notes of the material.

Information and communication technology has already changed many aspects of the way people work, relax and live their lives. Mobile computer equipment has enabled people to work in many different locations. It is now a familiar sight to see someone working on a train using a notebook computer. Many companies practise 'hot desking' where staff do not have a permanent desk but simply plug their notebook into the organisation's network and use mobile phones to communicate.

For many people the world wide web is the preferred way of arranging a holiday, booking theatre tickets, buying books and planning many aspects of their lives. You do not need to find reference books or send for leaflets. Searching the web to locate a relevant site has replaced these actions. There is no need to visit the supermarket since you can shop online and have the groceries delivered to your door.

Communication technology has assisted the development of a new type of community – a community of interest where members share a common need or interest. They may share a genetic illness and seek to discuss new medical developments or support each other. Other communities have an interest in collecting antiques, in military history, in tracing their family history and so on.

Information and communication technology is still a new development so more change is likely to result. The difficulty lies in predicting what the changes or impact will be.

Discussion

My own efforts are shown below. Your own work will be different, since notes are a personal record of the content so will depend on individual experience and understanding.

Information and communication technology has already **changed** many aspects of **the way people work, relax and live their lives**. Mobile computer equipment has enabled people **to work in many different location**s. It is now a familiar sight to see someone working on a train using a notebook computer. Many

➔

▶ Reading

Reading is a core part of learning. During a course you will be asked to read books, handouts, research papers and many other forms of written material including webpages. The key to effective reading is to understand why you are reading the material. What are you trying to achieve?

companies practise 'hot desking' where staff do not have a permanent desk but simply plug their notebook into the organisation's network and use mobile phones to communicate.

For many people the **world wide web is the preferred wa**y of arranging a holiday, booking theatre tickets, buying books and planning many aspects of their lives. You do not need to find reference books or send for leaflets. **Searching the web to locate a relevant site** has replaced these actions. There is no need to visit the supermarket since you can shop online and have the groceries delivered to your door.

Communication technology has assisted the development of a **new type of community** – a community of **interest** where members share a common need or interest. They may share a genetic illness and seek to discuss new medical developments or support each other. Other communities have an interest in collecting antiques, in military history, in tracing their family history and so on.

Information and communication technology is still a new development so more change is likely to result. The **difficulty lies in predicting** what the changes or impact will be.

An alternative approach is a spider graph:

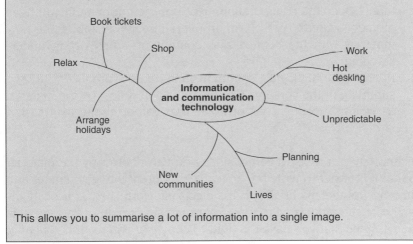

This allows you to summarise a lot of information into a single image.

Process

There are many reasons for reading (e.g. for pleasure). When you are studying your aim is to understand the content and how it relates to your studies. The process described below encourages you to approach reading in a systematic and active way. Casual reading will often be ineffective in that you will lose concentration, be easily distracted or fail to understand. Some useful tips to include in an active reading approach are:

1. Opening and closing paragraphs, or pages in longer documents, often give the objectives of the material and summarise its content, so it is useful initially to read them both to gain a clear insight into the material.
2. The abstract and conclusion of a paper will give you the main topics of the publication.
3. Written material is usually structured by means of headings, so an initial review of these will provide you with an overview of the content.
4. Browse the material to develop your overview. It is useful to consider illustrations, tables of information or lists since these will often be associated with key issues.
5. Read the material identifying the main points (i.e. highlight key points, write comments in the margin or use a notebook to record the important issues).
6. Reflect on the content by comparing it against what you have already studied and understand. Are you convinced by the argument? Does the content support or oppose information you have already located? Try to form an overall image by linking the new material with the context and content of your existing understanding.
7. Review your highlights, comments and notes to produce your own summary of the content. This will help you reflect on the material as well as develop a set of notes that will be useful for revision later.

Technology can assist reading, since you can photocopy the material so that it is easier to write on, or scan the content into a computer and turn the printed material into an electronic form that can be highlighted or cut and pasted to form your own set of notes. However, this does assume that you have the right to copy it. If you read the opening pages of the majority of books they severely limit the copying of the content (e.g. a publication cannot be copied, saved onto a computer or reproduced in any form without the permission of the copyright owner). You should study the copyright conditions in the text you are reading to check what you are able to do with the content. Colleges and libraries will usually provide you with guidance on what you can do. In many cases, you can copy content for personal educational use.

Reading online
Reading online content is similar to reading printed material, but

online material is designed in a very different way to a book. It is based on the concept of hypertext, that is, linking ideas together rather than producing a simple linear presentation of the information. By following the links you can find out more about a particular topic, but at the expense of moving away from the webpage on which you began. This can lead to confusion because it is sometimes difficult to know where you are. Links can be within a single website or to other websites, so it is easy to become lost. Links can be text, pictures or any other object that appears on the screen. Any combination of link is possible (e.g. text to text, text to picture, picture to picture or picture to text). Figure 2.2 illustrates hypertext links.

Hypertext links will often take you into the middle of a webpage and into the heart of a website making it difficult to be aware of the context of the rest of the site or even of the page. You are dependent on the designers of the site and their analysis of the material rather than your own if you simply follow the links and take no other action.

Many people find reading from a screen display more difficult than reading printed material. This is due, to some extent, to the lower quality of the text displayed compared to print. It is therefore good practice to avoid presenting large volumes of text on the screen, but to use illustrations, bullet point lists of information and short sentences. If a large volume of text is needed, it should be in a form that can be printed out if the reader desires to do so.

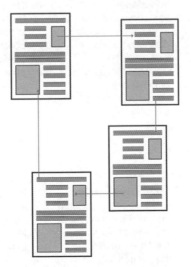

Figure 2.2   Hypertext

The reading process for a printed publication needs to be adapted for the different nature of the website and webpage. Table 2.1 compares a traditional printed document with a webpage.

Table 2.1 Comparison – printed publication and web content

Printed publication	Website	Comments
Read opening and closing paragraphs or pages to gain objectives and summary of the content.	The home page provides an overview of the site and many designers provide summaries throughout the material. Some websites have site maps, introductions and help facilities that offer an overview of content and structure. In some cases an introductory tour is offered to new users. Hypertext links make identifying opening and closing sections difficult.	Content is hidden within websites compared to printed publications so it is critical to gain a clear overview about what the site contains before embarking on reading the content. Consider the home page, site maps, introductions and tours to gain an insight into the material.
Written material is usually structured using headings, so an initial review of them will provide you with an overview of the content.	Websites are highly structured using headings to break a presentation into distinct sections. Hypertext links are also part of the structure, so need to be explored to gain an overview of the site.	Hypertext structure can be complex but good practice is to provide a consistent set of links following a distinct pattern. It is therefore useful to identify the approach taken. Site maps and early exploration can often help identify the approach.
Browse the material to develop your overview.	Browsing is a normal approach to considering a website. Rapidly jump around the site to explore the content. Illustrations are an important part of the information, so make an effort to study them.	Websites are a visual medium so that illustrations, graphical devices and structured text (e.g. tables) are important elements.

→

Remember that pages are frequently longer than a book page and some content will require you to scroll down or up to locate it.

Read the material identifying the main points (i.e. highlight key points, write comments in the margin or use a notebook to record the important issues).

Read with a purpose. Links will help you follow a theme but can also lead to you missing the rest of the content on a page so consider the whole content.

Make notes and if you find it helps, print the page and highlight and annotate it.

Webpages can be saved as an electronic document so that you can electronically highlight content or produce word processed notes.

Reflect on the content by comparing it against what you have already studied and understand. Are you convinced by the argument? Does the content support or oppose information you have already located? Try to form an overall image by linking the new material with the context and content of your existing understanding.

Reflection is vital to help you understand, so critically consider the content. Compare it against other sources.

Remember that almost anyone can launch a website, so the quality of the content may not be assured.

Review your highlights, comments and notes to produce your own summary of the content. This will help you reflect on the material as well as developing notes which will help your revision later

Review is again a key process in reading for learning.

It is important to record the URL (i.e. address) of the website so that you can find it again.

Remember that websites are dynamic. Their content continually changes so that it is useful if including a reference to a website to give the date when you read (accessed) it.

Activity   Reading online

Visit the British Library website at www.bl.uk/. Identify the information and resources that are provided for science and technology, or your own subject, and develop a short summary of the main elements of the resources. Explore the proposed reading process, perhaps comparing reading on the screen with printed webpages. Consider the British Library copyright statement.

Discussion

Websites are dynamic, so it is likely that the British Library site that you have looked at has been developed since I studied its contents. However, you should have noticed that:

1. The home page, site map and introductions provide good overviews of the site.
2. Many different groups of resources are provided by the British Library in relation to science and technology. These include:

   (a) electronic sources,
   (b) electronic databases,
   (c) electronic journals,
   (d) collections,
   (e) publications.

3. Some resources are not available online, but only from the library itself.

Websites are often covered by copyright (i.e. they are owned), so it is important to check what the owner of the site will allow you to do with the content. Many sites have copyright statements at the foot of each webpage or offer links to the webmaster who manages the site so that you can ask questions or seek permission to copy the material. In many cases, if you are simply copying the content for your personal study, you will be given permission. Your college or training provider should be able to advise you.

▶ Writing

When you write as part of a course of study, it is quite different from other forms of writing. You are seeking to show that you understand the subject through your writing. This requires that you:

- demonstrate a systematic and logical approach to the question you are answering;
- use evidence from your studies to support your case effectively;

- show a clear understanding of the topic (e.g. uses technical terms correctly);
- present the argument objectively (i.e. sometimes in the third person);
- analyse the evidence and do not simply present everything that you have read or heard.

This approach to writing is the same whether you are using a pen or a word processing application on a computer. That said, word processing provides you with distinct benefits. Writing with a pen, then redrafting your assignment or essay is a significant task, whereas with a word processor redrafting it is a straightforward task and a natural part of writing with a computer.

If you are writing an essay with a pen, you may well follow the approach below:

- notes;
- rough draft;
- final draft.

Each step requires a significant amount of time and is liable to error in that it involves copying previous work. Word processing also involves the same steps, but they are all part of a continuous process that does not require you to copy, thereby reducing the potential for mistakes. You can also add a fourth or even fifth stage in which you revise your essay. Revisions can be undertaken quickly so that you can improve your work.

There are further advantages with word processing, such as spelling and grammar checking, an electronic thesaurus and the ability to add extra ideas late in the writing process, which can be difficult to do with a handwritten document. Illustrations can be added to the text with little effort and blended accurately into the text. A handwritten document would require you to draw the illustration or to glue a photograph or other item into the document. You can produce a high-quality document which, unless you have excellent handwriting, is difficult to match by hand.

► Self-assessment

In all forms of learning it is important to be able to assess your own performance. This allows you to seek help when you need it or to make an extra effort when required. On conventional courses, you have many opportunities to judge your progress. These include:

- feedback from your assignment marker;
- comparing the outcomes of different assignments, since this will help you to evaluate what is required;
- sharing results with other learners;
- tutor feedback, both to you individually and to the whole group;
- listening to the answers to other learners' questions;
- discussions with other learners both formally and informally (in the corridor);
- deadlines provide a way of assessing your ability to keep up with the pace of the course;
- reflecting on your own efforts – are you making sufficient effort? Be honest with yourself. You are often provided with information about what the course designers expect from you (e.g. number of hours that you should study each week) so you can check your own workrate.

There are a variety of sources of information to help you assess your performance. Many of them involve face-to-face contact with tutors or other learners. This is absent from online courses. Other sources are available, but do require more individual action and acceptance of responsibility. In both cases, it is vital that you take advantage of your tutors by asking them questions, keeping them informed of your problems and requesting feedback. It is rarely enough to speak only to your tutor when you want an extension to a deadline.

e-Learning courses require a more proactive approach to self-assessment than equivalent conventional courses. However, many features are still available to you. Your work will be marked and feedback provided. You need to consider this feedback and ask for an explanation if you need it. It is more difficult to ask other learners informally how they have done, but email groups do allow you share information. If you share your results and thoughts then you will find that others will reveal theirs, since they also need to judge their own progress.

▶ Research skills

On all courses there is a need for learners to be able to find, interpret, compare and analyse information. This is, essentially, research.

An e-learning course is no different from a convention one in this respect, except that the learners can access a huge library of information without leaving their desks through the world wide web. The scale of this resource makes research skills more important, as you have far more information to consider and you must be the judge of its suitability. You can be overwhelmed with information.

Locating information
Regardless of what you are learning you will need the skills of finding information and assessing if it is suitable for your purpose. This may simply involve understanding how the college or public library works so that you can locate books and journals. However, even this task has more depth than initially appears. You need to judge the contents of the publication. Is it suitable for your needs? Is it up to date? Does it cover your subject at the correct level?

In order to answer these types of questions you need to be able to:

- analyse information;
- assess content;
- compare alternative sources.

One approach to assessing the suitability of a book quickly in a library or bookshop is to:

- Review the contents page – does it cover areas that you are interested in?
- Look up keywords in the index and consider how the book covers one area you know about – this will help you assess the approach and quality of the book.
- Check the publication date – some subjects are fairly dynamic, so a book more than a few years old will be unsuitable.
- Check the author – is he or she on your course reading list?

The skill of locating a book within a library is often dependent on your skill in using the library catalogue. These are frequently available on the college network or website and will allow you to search for books or papers without leaving home. This can save you time travelling to the library to search for a book that is already out on loan to another learner. Many libraries offer training programmes, awareness sessions or printed guides to help you to use the library effectively and you should take advantage of these. Each library will vary in the

---

Activity   Library catalogue

The Library of Congress catalogue is available online at http://catalog.loc.gov/. Visit the site and explore what kind of services are provided.

Discussion

There are several collection catalogues available to you and two different types of search that you can undertake (i.e. basic and guided searches). You can search in a variety of ways depending on how much you know about the information you are seeking, including searching by:

1. author's name;
2. title;
3. key words.

You can browse the resulting lists of entries and, by clicking on them, find out more information such as the full title of the book, its availability, etc. If you are a registered user of the library, you can request items.
  These types of services are offered by many college libraries. Check your own.

---

services and access to catalogues it offers, but a key success factor for all learners is to become competent in using the library.

Library catalogues and literature CD-ROMs

Many library catalogues or literature databases are provided on the library network or CD-ROMs. Searching these resources is not dissimilar to searching an online database. They are all slightly different, but many follow a similar pattern. Often the catalogue or literature database will offer several ways of searching it. A well-used approach is to allow you to search by:

- author;
- title;
- ISBN – this is a unique number found on the back of the title page of most books;
- subject;
- keyword.

Example:

- If you search for a particular author, you will be presented with a list

Activity   Searching for a book

Visit the Amazon online bookshop at www.amazon.com or www.amazon.co.uk and search for a book relevant to your course. It is useful to consider a range of alternative descriptions such as e-learning, online learning, computer-based learning, etc. Try a number of different searches and compare the results.

Select a few of the titles and investigate their contents, readers' reviews and authors' comments.

Discussion

All websites are dynamic, so your experience may be different from mine. You should have noticed the differences between searches using different terms. In the example, I found:

1. e-Learning – 913 titles located
2. online learning – 111 titles located
3. computer-based learning – 84 titles located

As well as some overlap between the lists, there were also considerable differences. It is always important to consider alternative ways of describing the topic so that you do not miss useful information.

The lists of books are displayed in order of their popularity, with the top three books shown separately. If you select a title you are presented with a physical description (e.g. length, hard- or soft-back, publisher and date of publication), a description of the book, reviews from readers and, sometimes, content pages and example chapters. Occasionally, lists of books are suggested relating to your topic but produced by Amazon customers. These can be useful if one of the lists is compiled by someone with similar needs to your own.

of the books or other items written by authors with that name. You then review the list to identify the one you are seeking.

Online bookshops

If you are buying a book from an online bookshop, you will sometimes be able to review contents pages and selected chapters in the way you can with a physical book. In addition, many books have readers' reviews and author's comments. Virtual bookshops often have enormous stocks, making searching for a book the equivalent of visiting a large library.

Research evidence

It is not sufficient to locate information and evidence. You need to be able to assess its appropriateness and suitability to your work. This is sometimes termed 'critical reviewing'. All information, regardless of its source (e.g. book, research paper or website) needs to be considered. If a document has been published, the content has been through some form of checking and assessment process. Many journals only publish papers after they have been assessed by other researchers working in the same field. This is know as peer reviewing and is a quality assurance process to ensure the paper is suitable for publication. Websites can be developed by anyone, so it is essential to check their quality. Later we will consider searching for information on the world wide web in more detail and how to assess its quality.

Critically reviewing information involves a variety of steps, including consideration of:

- the source of the publication (e.g. government survey, peer reviewed research paper, university research centre, recognised expert, thesis, etc.);
- the basis of the information (e.g. research findings, personal opinions, etc.);
- how well the information relates to other sources you have located; whether it is radically different from other evidence or supported by it;
- when the evidence was published – many subjects are continually developing, so only recent information is likely to be appropriate

It is essential that you do not accept everything you read as accurate. You must actively challenge the information and make a decision about its suitability.

Numerical data

Table 2.2 shows some data about climate (i.e. average rainfall, hours of sunshine, percentage of cloud cover and wind speed in the four quarters of the year). A useful skill is the ability to interpret this type of numerical information. The table assists your understanding by presenting the data in a systematic way, but it is still quite difficult to identify trends or to compare the different quarters. A more effective way is to present the data in a visual way (e.g. histogram, pie chart, etc.). Figure 2.3 illustrates the rainfall information in Table 2.2 as a pie chart comparing the four quarters. Figure 2.4 shows all the data presented as a line graph, so you can see and compare all the information.

Charts and graphs are quickly and effectively produced from tables

Table 2.2   Weather data by quarter

	1st Quarter	2nd Quarter	3rd Quarter	4th Quarter
Rainfall (inches)	12	34	17.0	11
Sunshine (hours)	6	3	4.5	7
Cloud (% of sky)	25	45	18.0	12
Wind speed (m.p.h.)	4	11	15.0	6

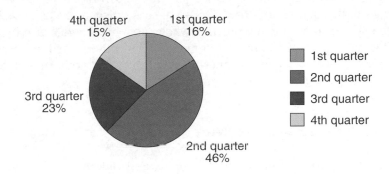

Figure 2.3   Rainfall

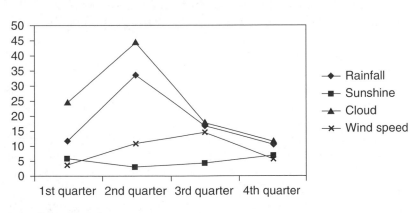

Figure 2.4   Climate data

produced in Microsoft Excel. These allow you to investigate and present information effectively. Although you could draw the charts and graphs using paper and pen, Microsoft Excel allows you to consider quickly a wide range of charts and graphs, thus letting you explore the best way of presenting and analysing the data.

Synthesis

A critical part of any learning process is synthesis, that is, combining and integrating information from several sources, with your own analysis. When you write an essay, undertake an assignment or simply make notes from a series of sources you are synthesising the data. Word processing and other applications are helpful when you are trying to integrate several sources. If you are handwriting an essay you may work through several drafts to produce a finished product. Each draft requires that you rewrite the whole document while a word-processed document can be edited many times without the burden of rewriting. There is no limit to the number drafts and you are able to focus your effort on integration and analysis.

▶ Learning in face-to-face groups

When you learn in a group, there are several different activities in which you may participate. These include:

* listening to a lecture, presentation or tutorial;
* observing a demonstration;
* working with other learners to achieve a common goal;
* undertaking a practical activity (e.g. laboratory experiment).

This kind of learning involves the use of a range of skills such as listening, observing, co-operating, questioning and note taking. Probably one of the key benefits of a face-to-face learning activity is the opportunity to ask questions to clarify your understanding, establish links with other areas or simply because you are confused. A parallel benefit is that you can hear other learners' questions and the associated answers. It is obviously better to ask your questions as this will directly benefit your own needs, but on many occasions you have probably thought 'I wish I had asked that'.

e-Learning allows you to ask questions of your tutor using email and if these are shared through an electronic mailgroup or other form of online conferencing you can also benefit from your peers' questions. Many participants in mailgroups have found that they gain a great deal from reading the other messages. This is called 'vicarious learning' (Cox *et al.* 1999).

Face-to-face approaches can provide you with numerous opportunities for informal conversations – in the corridor, over refreshments and before and after the formal session. These are usually with fellow learners, but occasionally involve the tutor or lecturer, allowing you to check your understanding against that of your peers, seek help or on e-learning courses, there will be opportunities to informally discuss the course with your peers using chatrooms or mailgroups. These may be moderated by tutors who will offer advice or answer questions if they feel they need to intervene, but in some cases tutors are not permitted entry, letting you debate issues in private. Chatrooms and other forms of online discussion require you to take the initiative by sending a message and this can be a little strange at first, but participation will help you.

Face-to-face learning enables you to see what is happening with your tutor or peers. When you communicate by email you have no way of knowing what is going on at the other end. Your tutor or colleague may be ill, away on a trip or simply busy. We all expect an immediate response to an email message and it is often frustrating when you ask a question or request a change and nothing seems to happen. In face-to-face communication you can at least go along and find out what is wrong. Some email systems allow you to ask for a receipt when your message is opened, but some computer systems block receipts so this is not a guarantee. Nevertheless, when they are available they can at least reassure you that your message has arrived. Some courses have

Activity   Face-to-face learning

When you are next in a face-to-face group learning situation, note each question and answer, and reflect on how much you have gained from hearing the dialogue.

Discussion

You should be able to identify clearer benefits than simply being able to hear the discussion. Asking your own questions adds considerable value to the process since participation is not simply about passive listening. Your tutors gain from your questions in that they are able to adjust their presentation to ensure your understanding is more likely. Without feedback, tutors will naturally assume you understand. This applies to both face-to-face and e-learning courses.

published standards for replying to messages (e.g. within 24 hours) and this is a useful feature to check when you are considering a course.

▶ Stress

Learning can be a stressful process. You have deadlines to meet and assessments to pass. This can place considerable pressure on you. How you deal with stress in learning situations can depend on the support that you have available – not just the formal support of your tutor, although this is very important, but also the relatively informal help of other learners, your friends and family. This is true of all forms of learning, whether they be conventional or e-learning.

In face-to-face situations, your fellow learners and tutors will sometimes realise that you need assistance when your behaviour or demeanour is unusual. In the online environment this is more difficult to identify, so you need to take more responsibility to ensure that stress produced by learning pressures does not cause you too many problems. If you can identify the causes of stress you are better equipped to deal with it.

If you know what your main causes of stress are, you need to take action to reduce or eliminate them. Insufficient time to complete work is often a source of stress. This is frequently caused by poor time

Activity   Pressure

Consider your own experience of stress. When do you feel under pressure? What are the main causes of stress? Write a list of the main times when you feel pressured.

Discussion

You may feel stressed by:

1. approaching assessment (e.g. examinations);
2. missing deadlines;
3. getting behind with studying;
4. time pressure;
5. studying new material;
6. finding the subject difficult to understand;
7. being unsure of what is expected of you;
8. the challenge of new methods (e.g. e-learning);
9. work pressures.

management. In face-to-face learning the responsibility for time management is divided between you and your tutor. They will often remind you of deadlines and encourage you to start work at the appropriate moment. e-Learning courses are likely to place more responsibility for managing your time on you. In later chapters you will consider the time management skills you need as an e-learner. However, some of the general points to consider are:

• being systematic in your approach to learning;
• 'a little and often' approach is usually better than trying to do too much with long intervals between studying;
• plan your time by considering what is required and when you need to do it.

► Summary

1. **Notes**
   e-Learning courses provide most of the content as text and you can save or print it. This appears to do away with the need to take notes, but there is the risk that you will record everything yet study very little of it. It is vital to read and analyse the material. You can annotate and highlight electronic documents, which will assist you during revision months later by identifying the key points.

2. **Reading**
   Online reading material is structured differently to printed publications. Online text is based on the concept of hypertext, that is, concepts are linked together rather than presented as a linear flow of information. To read more about an idea you need to follow the links.

   It is important when reading hypertext documents that you initially gain an appreciation of the content and structure. The home page of a website will often provide an overview and some websites have site maps, introductions and help facilities which will also aid you.

3. **Writing**
   Writing in any form of study is concerned with showing your understanding of the subject. This is the same whether you are using a pen or a word processing application, although word-

processing does give some additional benefits (i.e. redrafting assignments, spelling and grammar checking and thesaurus facilities).

Writing is the main communication method of e-learning.

4. **Self-assessment**
    It is important to be able to assess your performance in all forms of learning. This is especially true of e-learning in that you are often working at a distance from your tutor or peers so there is less opportunity for informal assessment.

    You need to be proactive to self-assessment using assignment marks and feedback, but also asking for explanations from your tutor or enquiring how your peers are doing.

5. **Research Skills**
    All forms of learning require you to be able to find, interpret, compare and analyse information. This requires you to be able find information (e.g. use a library and search the world wide web) and judge its appropriateness. A key skill is the use of a library catalogue. This is often available on a college's computer network or on CD-ROM. Libraries will usually help you to understand how to use them effectively.

    Judging the suitability of information requires consideration of the source and basis of the publication, how well the information relates to other sources and when the evidence was published.

    An important way of considering numerical information is to use charts and graphs.

    Learning requires you to synthesise information by combining and integrating information from several sources. Word processing is very helpful when you are trying to integrate several sources.

6. **Learning in face-to-face groups**
    When you are learning in a group, you are using a range of skills such as listening, observing, co-operating, questioning and note taking. A benefit of face-to-face learning is the opportunity to ask questions and hear the answers to other peoples' questions. A similar opportunity exists in e-learning through the use of email or other forms of computer mediated communication.

    Face-to-face approaches give you the opportunity for informal conversations to check your understanding or judge your own performance. e-Learning requires more formality in that you need to send an email or use a chatroom.

7. **Stress**

   All forms of learning can be stressful. e-Learning is potentially more demanding because you are responsible for your own learning. If you can identify the causes of stress you are better equipped to deal with it.

3 Computer Skills

In order to be a successful e-learner you need to have a good range of basic computer skills. Computers are good for keeping records, presenting information and manipulating data – all fundamental requirements of any form of education. Communication technology provides additional advantages by allowing you to locate sources of information on the world wide web or within the college's online resources as well as being able to quickly communicate with tutors and other learners. This chapter assumes that you have used a computer for tasks such as word processing and using a spreadsheet. It aims to help you develop the skills that you will need as a learner. It covers:

- assessing your skills;
- accessibility;
- file management;
- compressing files;
- tracking changes;
- saving and backing up your information;
- applications;
- searching the world wide web;
- assessing the quality of online information;
- presenting information (i.e. tables, charts and graphs);
- transferring information;
- digital images;
- plagiarism;
- copyright;
- utilities.

► Assessment of skills

A useful place to start is to consider your existing skills. The activity below provides you with a straightforward table to assess your competency.

Activity   Assessment information and communication skills

Assess your skills and understanding against the simple structure shown in Table 3.1. These are the skills that form the basis of this chapter. They are a mixture of the practical skills and technical knowledge that you need for e-learning. If you would like to undertake a more detailed assessment of your ICT skills, you will find a more comprehensive checklist in Appendix B.

Table 3.1   Skills assessment

Skills	Competence		
	Poor	*Acceptable*	*Excellent*
Adjusting the operating system to meet your personal preferences and needs			
Filing systems			
File formats			
Applications			
Computer memory			
Compressing files			
Searching the world wide web			
Judging the quality of online content			
Presenting information (charts and graphs)			
Working with numbers			
CD-RW			
USB storage			
Digital images			
Copyright			

Discussion

There are a wide range of ICT courses and books available to you. They can help you develop your skills and knowledge. Your college and employer may offer opportunities to develop your ICT skills.

▶ Windows accessibility options

Microsoft Windows provides users with a range of options to help to make the system more accessible for you. These include:

- Changing the contrast of the display to making reading easier
- StickyKeys allow you to press one key at a time rather than having to press multiple keys to enact a function.
- FilterKeys allow you to instruct the system to overlook repeated key presses.
- ToggleKeys instructs the system to play a tone when pressing the capital, number or scroll lock keys.
- SoundSentry instructs the system to display a warning when it makes a noise.
- ShowSounds instructs the system to show a message when it uses speech or sounds.
- Cursor blink rates and width can be controlled so that the pointer is more visible.
- The mouse pointer can be contolled with the keyboard number pad for users who find controlling a mouse difficult.

These features can be accessed by selecting the Control Panel Option in the Start menu. This will open the Control Panel window where you

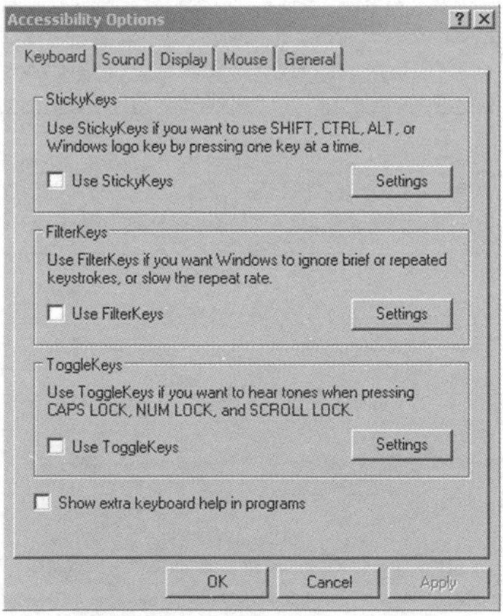

Figure 3.1   Accessibility options

Activity   Accessibility options

Click on the Start button to reveal the menu containing the Control Panel option. Click on Control Panel to reveal its window and then on the Accessibility option. The Accessibility window (Figure 3.1) will appear. Explore what happens when you select:

1. the high contrast option (i.e. select the Display tab in the Accessibility window and click in the radio button to show a tick and then on the OK button). To return to the original settings, repeat the process and click again in the radio button, which will remove the tick.
2. the ToggleKeys option (i.e. select the Keyboard tab in the Accessibility window and click in the radio button to show a tick and then on the OK button). Press the capital, number and scroll lock keys. To return to the original settings, repeat the process and click again in the radio button, which will remove the tick.

Remember to return the system to the original settings when you complete this exercise.

Discussion

1. When high contrast is chosen, the system asks you initially to wait before it alters the colours to maximise contrast (e.g. black on white) and increases the size of characters so the labels are larger.
2. When you press the capital, number and scroll lock keys you will hear a noise to indicate they have been pressed.

can see the Accessibility options icon or file name. If you click the Accessibility option then a window opens providing you with access to the range of choices (Figure 3.1).

Mouse

One accessibility option that is very useful is to make the mouse suitable for a left-handed person. If you click on the Start button and select the Control Panel option, it will reveal the Control Panel window. If you select the mouse icon, it will open the Mouse Properties window. Under the button tab is the radio button to switch the mouse buttons around to make it suitable for a left-handed user.

The Mouse Properties window also provides options for you to adjust:

- the double clicking speed;
- the pointer;
- the mouse wheel.

▶ File management

Computers provide a means for storing vast amounts of information. The world wide web adds to this ability by offering enormous volumes of data that you can save electronically. Potentially you should not have a problem with a shortage of information. Often the dilemma is that you have too much. Information is not useful unless you can quickly locate it. It is important to have an efficient and effective filing system, that is, one that is:

- **Meaningful** – names of files and folders that are easy to recognise so information can be located in a straightforward way.
- **Clearly structured** – simple, consistent and clear. Too many files and folders can make location more difficult.

To create a filing system in Microsoft Windows you need to employ Windows Explorer. This can be opened by selecting the Start button, highlighting the Programs option to reveal the list of applications and then highlighting the Accessories item to show a sub-menu that includes Windows Explorer. The location of applications does depend on the operating system and how the system is configured, so this may be slightly different on your computer. Click on Windows Explorer and the application will open (Figure 3.2). Figure 3.2 shows my own folders. The display is divided into two areas. The left-hand side shows a list of folders, while the right-hand side shows the detailed contents of the

Activity   File management

Consider e-learning skills – what folders and structure would you need to cover this subject? Develop a filing system that is meaningful and clear.

Discussion

It is likely that this filing system will only be part of an overall system, so a master folder called e-Learning Skills is appropriate. Within this folder a range of sub-folders can be created to cover issues such as:

1. traditional skills;
2. computer skills;
3. communication skills;
4. group and co-operative learning;
5. other resources.

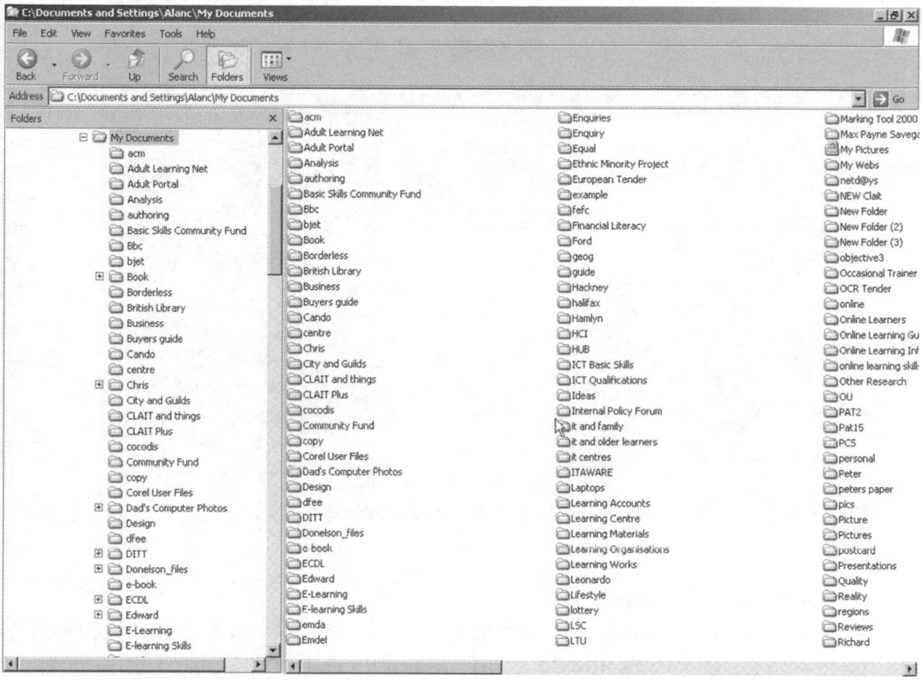

Figure 3.2 Windows Explorer

selected folder (My Documents – highlighted on the left). When a folder has a plus sign beside it, this indicates that it contains other folders.

When you use a computer regularly you will rapidly produce a large number of folders, so it is important to understand how to use the Explorer functions to maintain your files and folders. The main functions are:

- New (create a new folder);
- Delete a file or folder;
- Rename a file or folder;
- Cut, copy and paste (copy or move files and folders);
- Drag and drop (move files and folders using the mouse – alternative to copying and pasting).

Figure 3.3 shows the main maintenance functions available in the File and Edit menus.

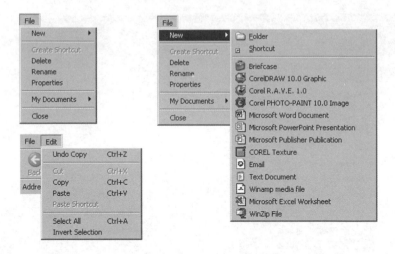

Figure 3.3 Maintenance functions – File and Edit menu

Create a new folder

To create a new folder, select the File menu, highlight the New option to reveal a sub-menu and click on the Folder option (Figure 3.3). A new folder will appear in the right-hand area of the Explorer application with the name New Folder highlighted. You need to enter a name for the folder from the keyboard. If you want to create a folder within an existing folder then initially you highlight the existing folder, by clicking on it.

Delete a file or folder

Highlight the folder or file by clicking on it with the mouse pointer, select the File menu, by clicking on it in the same way, and then click on the Delete option. A message will appear asking you to confirm that you want to remove the folder you have deleted. This safeguards you against deleting files or folders in error.

Rename a file or folder

Highlight the folder or file, select the File menu and click on the Rename option. The folder's or file's existing name will be highlighted and you can enter a new name from the keyboard.

Cut, copy and paste

Highlight the folder or file you want to cut or copy, select the Edit menu

Activity   File system

Using Windows Explorer create the file system you designed earlier for Electronic Learning Skills.

Discussion

My effort is shown in Figure 3.4:

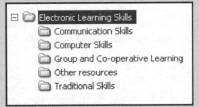

Figure 3.4   File structure

I have created a master folder called Electronic Learning Skills and then, within this folder, a series of sub-folders.

and click on the Copy or Cut options. Move your cursor or pointer to the folder that you want to copy or move the file or folder to and then select the Paste option in the Edit menu. The cut option moves the file or folder permanently, while the copy function leaves the original file or folder in place.

Drag and drop

Highlight the folder or file and by holding down the left mouse button while the pointer is on the highlighted file you can drag the file or folder to a new position. Let go of the mouse button to leave the file in its new position. If you place a dragged file or folder over an existing folder, you can insert it into the folder. This is an alternative to cutting and pasting.

▶ File formats

All computer information is provided in the form of files, that is, a collection of similar information (e.g. text, pictures, etc.). It is important that you are able to distinguish between different files, since this will

.xls - Microsoft Excel Spreadsheet File
.ZIP - WinZip Compressed File
.doc - Microsoft Word Wordprocessing File
.rtf - Rich Text File - Wordprocessing File
.txt - Text File - Wordprocessing File
.GIF - GIF Image File
.pdf - Adobe Acrobat File
.bmp - Bitmap Image File
.htm - Webpage File and Microsoft FrontPage File
.ppt - Microsoft PowerPoint
.pub - Microsoft Publisher - Desktop Publishing
.mdb - Microsoft Access Database File

Figure 3.5 File formats extensions and icons

allow you to select what is suitable for particular applications and uses. In Microsoft Windows, files are given extensions (e.g. '.doc', '.xls', etc.) to their names depending on the type of data they contain. This lets you locate them quickly. In addition, an icon is added to assist with identification (Figure 3.5).

Microsoft Windows allows you to change the layout and display of files. One of the most useful options is Details. This provides you with information about the nature of the file. Within Windows Explorer, select the View menu and click on the Details option. Figure 3.6 shows the available View options.

Figure 3.7 shows the Detail display. It offers you information on:

- name of file;
- size of file;
- type of file;
- date file was last modified.

This is important information that can help you identify and use the files.

Adobe Acrobat

Adobe Acrobat is a document file format that is widely used on the internet for disseminating publications. Such files can be identified by the extension .pdf – portable document format. In order to read these files you need to use the Adobe Reader application. This is a free application widely distributed on websites. You can obtain a copy from www.adobe.com. If you need to create Adobe Acrobat files you must purchase the full system.

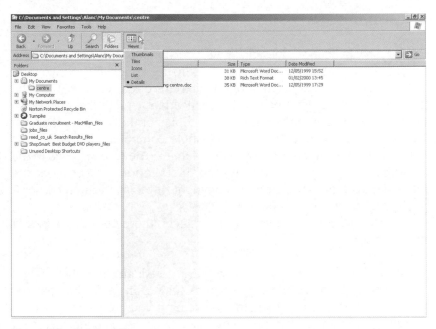

Figure 3.6   Details option

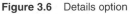

Figure 3.7   Details display

▶ Applications

Buying an application does not give you complete rights to use the product in any way you like. When you install an application, you are agreeing to the seller's conditions which are often referred to as the licence. This limits your use of the application. One of the key conditions is a restriction on the number of copies of the software that you can install. This is often limited to a single computer. Each licence is different, so it is important that you read them. They are included in the packaging or displayed during the installation process on the computer. You are infringing the copyright of the application owner if you break the licence conditions.

Apart from commercial software products, there are other types of products:

- **Shareware** products that allow you to evaluate them before you purchase them. They are sometimes limited in their functionality, but once you agree to buy the application you are supplied with a full version and sometimes a manual. Their use is controlled by a licence.
- **Freeware** or open source applications, which are free and frequently do not limit your use of them. Often, the only condition is that you acknowledge their source but normally no formal support is available.

A key difference between commercial, shareware and freeware products is the degree of technical support available. Commercial products usually provide support, shareware sometimes does, and freeware almost always does not have links to formal support, although other users will sometimes help you if you can locate them.

Before you use or buy any product it is important to check the following details:

- What conditions govern its use? Read the licence and ask the seller or supplier for information.
- What system requirements the product requires (e.g. type of processor, random access memory and storage). Many suppliers will provide this in two forms:

    (a) the minimum requirements to operate the application (e.g. the program may run slowly),

(b) the recommended requirements (e.g. the optimum level needed to run the application).

Many e-learning providers offer advice on what hardware and soft-ware you will need to undertake their courses.

▶ Compressing files

Sending or moving files between computer systems appears to be a straightforward task and in many cases it is. However, if the file is so large that it cannot fit on a floppy disk or it will take a long time to send over the internet, then it can be more difficult. Some email systems limit the size of attachments and large files are not accepted. If you are sending an email with a large attachment to someone's home PC, it may take them a long time to download it, effectively blocking their email system. This will not make you popular!

One method of overcoming the problem is to compress the file (i.e. squeeze it down into a smaller size). One of the best known of several compressing products is WinZip, a tool to compress files for Microsoft Windows. The process of compressing files is now often called zipping. Currently, you can download an evaluation version of WinZip from their website at http://www.zinwip.com/ to assess if it is suitable for you. There are also a variety of compression tools that can be down-loaded from the world wide web. Some of these are shareware or public domain products.

Image files are frequently very large and computer users are often surprised by the size of a single picture. A bitmap file can occupy many megabytes of space. A file compression application and some paint or image editing applications offer ways to substantially reduce the size of image files. Another way is to change the image file format using an image application, but this will sometimes reduce the quality of the image.

▶ Saving and backing up your information

A common problem that almost every computer user has experienced is losing work. This does not have to happen. You need to develop your own good procedures to safeguard your work. The first basic step is to save your work regularly (i.e. every few minutes so that if the computer has a problem you only lose a few minutes work). Many applications can be set so that they will automatically save your work.

Example:

- Microsoft Word allows you to set the automatic save for a period of your own choice by selecting the Tools menu and clicking on the Options item to reveal the Options window. Within the Save tab are the options.

Saving your work will give you protection against temporary computer problems such as a power failure, but will not entirely protect you if there is a major problem such as a virus infection or permanent system failure. It is good practice to copy your entire set of files to a medium that you can move to another computer if your own computer has failed.

There are several ways of saving or backing up all your files, including copying files to:

- a CD-RW disc;
- a USB memory stick (dongle);
- a DVD RAM disc;
- magnetic tape.

You need to select the method that suits you best, but the key is to establish a system for regularly backing up your information. If a disaster occurs, you will lose any information added or amendments made to your files since you last made a backup. Thus a weekly backup means that you are risking a week's worth of information. A daily backup risks at most a day's worth. You need to decide what you are prepared to lose.

Devices

Transferring files between computers can involve the use of a CD-RW (Compact Disc – Read/Write) or USB memory stick (dongle).

A CD-RW is a compact disk formatted to allow you to save information on it. The CD-RW requires a special drive, which many computer systems are now fitted with as standard, and you can save hundreds of megabytes of information onto the disc. The CD-RW disc can then be taken to another computer with a CD-ROM drive and the information read from the disc.

A USB memory stick, or dongle, is a small device which you plug into the computer's USB port. It then becomes an extra disc on which you can save files. USB dongles are available in a variety of sizes (e.g. 16, 32, 64, 128 and 256 Mbytes). To move the saved files you simply unplug the dongle and then plug it into another computer's USB port.

A significant issue when transferring any files is viruses. Many college and training organisation computers have restrictions on the transferring of files because of the risk of infection. You should always check the files with your virus protection software before transferring them. It is possible to set up your protection system to check both incoming and outgoing files attached to emails, regularly check your whole system and those files stored on floppy, CD-ROM and DVD discs and a USB memory stick. This level of precaution is essential to prevent virus infection.

► Tracking changes

Group work is often a part of e-learning so you may find yourself working on a document with other learners. To help you with this process, Microsoft Word has a function within the Tools menu called Track Changes (Figure 3.8). This highlights the changes that one writer makes to a document so that partners can see what has been added. If the changes are accepted, you can add them to the document, either one at a time or all at once.

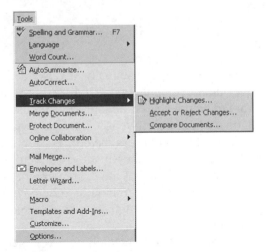

Figure 3.8 Track changes

▶ Searching and quality

The world wide web is an enormous information resource covering almost every subject that you are likely to be interested in. However, finding the information you require in the millions of websites that make up the web can be difficult. You have to be able to decide if the site's content is accurate, reliable and suitable for your purpose.

You need to develop two separate sets of skills:

1. searching for information;
2. judging the quality of information.

To help you locate information on the world wide web there are search engines, which are essentially large databases of webpages that have been created by the engine. The search engine indexes the webpages based on the words they contain. To find information you ask the engine to search the database for pages containing the keywords you have entered. The database rather than the web is searched, so it is very quick.

Types of search engine

There are a wide variety of search engines. All of them will locate information for you, but the way they operate does vary. There are three different types:

1. individual
2. meta
3. directory

An individual search engine is essentially as described above, while a meta engine does not develop its own database but searches the databases of several individual search engines. Both these types of engine will often provide a directory of websites linked to particular subjects (e.g. shopping, property, computers, health, etc.), normally based on the most popular types of searches made. A directory of websites is compiled and edited by the staff of the search engine and so this type will sometimes save you time searching as they have listed the main sites. There are some search engines that are specialist directory services (e.g. Yahoo).

Search engines allow you to search for a variety of resources including:

- webpages;
- images;
- discussion groups;
- news;
- individual email addresses.

There are many different search engines. Some of the larger ones are listed below:

AltaVista	http://altavista.com/
	www.uk.altavista.com/
AllThe Web.com	www.alltheweb.com
Ask Jeeves	www.askjeeves.com
Dogpile	www.dogpile.com/
Excite	www.excite.com/
Google	www.google.co.uk
HotBot	www.hotbot.com/
Looksmart	www.looksmart.com/
Lycos	www.uk.lycos.com/
MSN Search	http://search.msn.com
Metacrawler	www.metacrawler.com
Northern Lights	www.nlsearch.com/
Webcrawler	www.webcrawler.com/
Yahoo	www.yahoo.co.uk

Most people find it easy to search the web, but difficult to find exactly what they are seeking. Almost all search engines will provide help to users. You should always investigate the different options as they can save you time and effort. Search engines will locate information in different ways, so you will achieve different results if you use several engines.

Example – comparing different search engines:

- Locate webpages about climate warming using the Google and MSN Search engines. Enter 'Climate Warming' as keywords in both engines:
  - Google located 474 000 pages (Figure 3.9)
  - MSN Search located 63 pages (Figure 3.10)

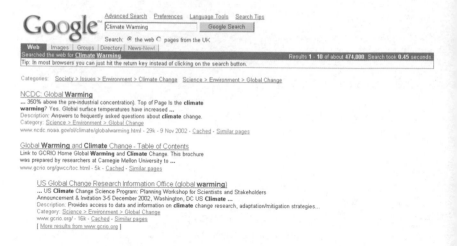

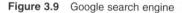

Figure 3.9   Google search engine

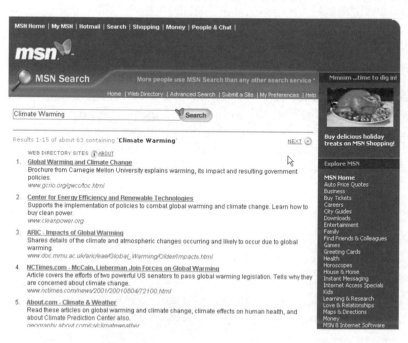

Figure 3.10   MSN search engine

- This is quite a difference. MSN Search uses editors to select sites so you are locating the sites that the editors feel are the most appropriate, whereas Google is presenting you with the many webpages that its database holds without editing. Another difference is that Google is searching for pages that contain both the *words* Climate and Warming but not necessarily in the order you have entered

Activity   Comparing search engines

Explore Google and MSN Search or two other search engines in order to compare the directories they hold, the help with searching, the services they provide and the types of search they offer (e.g. images, individual email addresses).

Discussion

My own experience is likely to be different from yours, since the world wide web is dynamic and in a state of continual change.

Both of these search engines are sophisticated tools and I will only describe some of their features to illustrate their services.

GOOGLE

This search engine offers a number of different ways of searching including:

1. webpages;
2. images;
3. usenet groups;
4. directories – 16 main categories of directories with many sub-categories;
5. news.

In addition, Google provides help with advanced searching techniques, languages and a wide range of specialist services.

MSN

This search engine is a specialist directory service, so it is structured in a different way to Google. It provides access to many directories through main headings such as:

1. news;
2. shopping;
3. money;
4. people and chat.

In addition, MSN also provides access to email accounts (i.e. hotmail) and chat groups.

them. If we enclose the words searched on Google in inverted commas – 'Climate Warming' – and search again, Google will match the *phrase* with pages, and in this case the number of hits is reduced to 12 200. Google has a facility that allows you to search within the matched sites and therefore to focus in on your precise needs.

- The world wide web is very volatile and dynamic, so it is likely that if you repeat this search a few days later you will get different detailed results, but the overall emphasis should be similar.

Keywords

How you enter your keywords will influence your search. Some search engines will assume you are searching for any of the words you have entered, while others will match pages that contain all the words in any order; some will match the exact phrase. You need to explore the engine to understand how it works. Even small changes in keywords can dramatically change the search results.

Some straightforward tips to improve your searching are:

- **Explore** – it often useful just to try some word(s) to see what results you get. This provides useful information that will help you to concentrate your search.
- **Be direct** – if you want to find out about rainfall in Lancashire, do not enter 'rainfall' but use 'Lancashire rainfall'.
- **Feedback** – sometimes search engines will give you feedback when a search has failed (e.g. that you have been too specific). Take notice of the feedback and alter your keywords accordingly.
- **Use the plus sign** to ensure that all the words you enter are present on the matched pages (e.g. +Lancashire +rainfall). Some search engines automatically match all the words you enter.
- **Use inverted commas** to match the exact phrase (e.g. 'Lancashire rainfall'). This is very specific and can sometimes result in very few or no matches.
- **Use the minus symbol** to eliminate pages containing information you do not need (e.g. +Lancashire +Rainfall –Snow will not match any page with snow).
- **You can combine symbols** (e.g. 'Lancashire rainfall' –Burnley will match pages with the exact phrase 'Lancashire rainfall' that do not contain the word Burnley, which is a town in Lancashire).

Activity   Keyword searching

Try locating information concerned with Lancashire rainfall using more than one search engine.

1. Enter Rainfall
2. Enter +Lancashire +rainfall
3. Enter 'Lancashire rainfall'
4. Enter +Lancashire +rainfall –snow

What were the results? Did the symbols have any effect (some search engines do not recognise symbols)?

Try some alternative keywords, such as Lancashire climate, Lancashire weather, etc. Try including the word 'rainfall'. What were the results?

Compare and contrast your results.

Discussion

I tried the searches in two engines: Lycos and Webcrawler. The results were:

LYCOS

1. Rainfall produced 61 696 hits
2. +Lancashire +rainfall produced 514 hits
3. 'Lancashire rainfall' produced no results
4. +Lancashire +rainfall –snow produced 436 results, showing the impact of eliminating pages with the word 'snow'

WEBCRAWLER

1. Rainfall produced 93 hits
2. +Lancashire +rainfall produced 59 hits
3. 'Lancashire rainfall' produced 20 hits
4. +Lancashire +rainfall –snow produced 55 results, showing the impact of eliminating pages with the word 'snow'

These results illustrate the importance of understanding your search engines so that you can maximise the possibilities of locating the information you seek.

Boolean searching

An alternative to using symbols in keyword searches is to employ Boolean logic. This is essentially the way you search databases. The world wide web is rather like a huge database. There are three Boolean logic operators:

1. OR
2. AND
3. NOT

If you were searching for information about Kings you might search for:

Kings OR Princes

This would match with pages that had at least one of the keywords (i.e. Kings or Princes). Alternatively you might use:

Kings AND Princes

This would match with pages that had both keywords. You might use also:

Kings NOT Princes

This would match only with pages that contained the keyword Kings but which did not have the keyword Princes.

Other tips
Some other tips for searching are:

- Each search engine has its own set of conditions so it is useful to explore the help function to find out how the engine operates.
- Some engines allow you to choose to search only UK sites and thus narrow down the search immediately. This is useful if you want to find specific UK information such as train times.
- Some engines allow you to search the results of an earlier search. This can be helpful when you are seeking to focus on a particular topic by refining the keywords.

Favorites
Once you have invested time in locating a useful site, the next step is to ensure that you can locate the site again. Internet Explorer and other browsers provide a function to save your sites so that you can rapidly visit them again. Figure 3.11 shows the Favorites menu in Internet Explorer. While you are visiting the site you want to save, select the Favorites menu and then the Add to Favorites option to reveal the Add

Activity   Boolean logic operators

Using a search engine of your choice undertake the following Boolean searches:

1. Kings OR Princes
2. Kings AND Princes
3. Kings NOT Princes

Also combine the Boolean operators with symbols so that:

4. Kings NOT Princes –Queens

Discussion

When the three keyword searches using the logic operators were entered into AltaVista search engine the following results were obtained:

1. Kings OR Princes – produced 1 723 679 matches
2. Kings AND Princes – produced 14 770 matches
3. Kings NOT Princes – produced 132 606 matches

You can also combine Boolean with symbols so that:

4. Kings NOT Princes –Queens – produced 128 603 matches, since it does not match with pages that contain the word Queens.

Your searches will probably have produced different results due to the dynamic nature of the world wide web and your choice of search engine.

Favorite window. You need to give the site an appropriate name. The system will suggest one based on the webpage and you can accept or change this name. You can also group your favorite sites into folders to help you organise them. Once you have been using the world wide web for a few months you will be surprised at the large number of favorites you have accumulated. It is therefore good practice to organise your favorites into folders and to give them names you will remember. To visit a favorite you simply open the Favorite menu and click on it. If you are online, the browser will then take you to the webpage within the site that you used to create the favorite.

Good practice with using favorites is to:

* use memorable names so that you can find the site again;
* organise your favorites into folders;
* edit your lists regularly to avoid confusion;
* remember you are saving links to individual pages rather than the site.

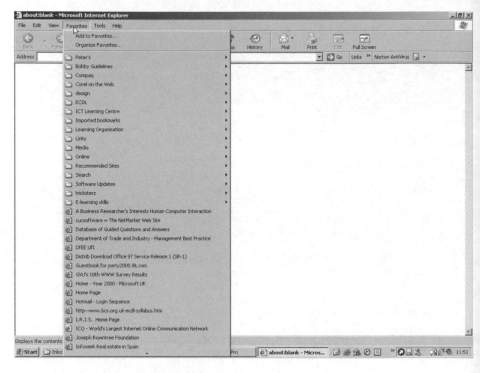

Figure 3.11   Favorite function on Internet Explorer

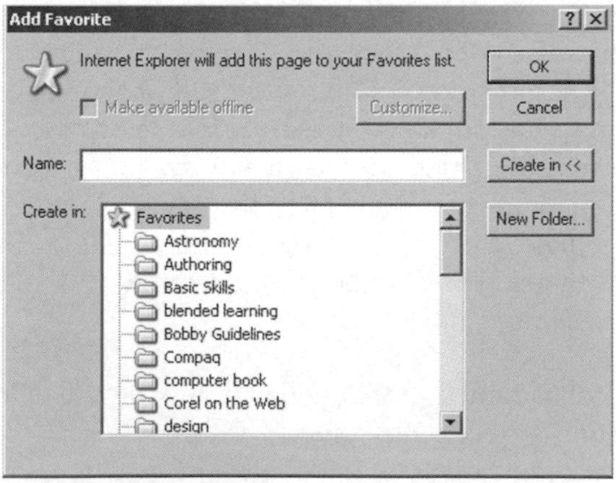

Figure 3.12   Add Favorites to Internet Explorer

If you are using Netscape as your browser, you will find that the favorite function is called Bookmark and operates in a similar way.

Judging the quality of websites

Once you have used a search engine to locate websites, you need to be able to assess the quality of the information that the site offers you. A search engine will present you with a list of webpages from which you can choose. You need to determine the quality and suitability of the information present on the pages.

Anyone can develop a website and put personal views on the pages. Your first step is to determine the quality of information by considering who produced the content. Is it a personal website – that is, one produced by an individual for presenting his or her interests/opinions? This is often shown by the website address or URL having an individual's name included in it (e.g. /Jbrown/) or being hosted by an Internet Service Provider that specialises in websites. You can determine this by jumping first to the home site (e.g. if the URL is www.homesite.co.uk/staff/sss99/Jbrown/ reduce this to www.homesite.co.uk). Some major hosting services include:

- www.geocities.com
- www.doteasy.com
- www.freeservers.com
- www.hypermarket.net

Information that is solely the opinion of one individual is limited in value and can be very misleading. Nevertheless, individual sites can be useful. In order to judge their value you need to know something about them. Does the site provide any information about the site author? For example, many academic researchers have individual sites that provide papers and information about their research. Often these sites give biographical information about the author that can give you a valuable insight into the quality of the content of the site.

The address of a website shows you the domain of the website owner (e.g. government, non-profit organisation, commercial organisation, educational establishment, etc.). These include:

- gov – government
- mil – military
- org – non-profit organisation
- edu – educational body

- ac – academic institution
- co or com – commercial company

Is the domain appropriate for the information presented and is there any vested interest involved (e.g. manufacturers of equipment providing information about their own products)? In some cases this kind of information is valuable and, if you are seeking the technical specification of a product, the manufacturer's website is an excellent place to look. However, marketing information is also often presented on many commercial sites.

There is a great deal on a webpage that you can use to assess quality. Who owns or is responsible for the page? You might find links called 'About' or 'Home Page'. These should take you to descriptions about the organisation or individual who published the site and help you to make judgements about the content. Some sites will allow you to contact the organisation or individual. There is often a link called 'Contact', enabling you to email the person responsible for the site.

If you cannot locate a link then you can reduce the URL (website address) by deleting parts of the address as shown earlier (e.g. from www.examplesite.co.uk/index/lld34/lord/ reduce to www.example-site.co.uk/) to enable you to return to the home page of the site. This should help you determine who the author of the material is. The key is to consider whether the organisation or individual is appropriate for the page content and whether they are likely to be putting forward an objective or a subjective viewpoint. You should be wary of subjective material.

Activity   Appropriate sites

Which of these sites is appropriate for the presented information? How would you judge the quality of the content?

- University site – content about scientific research;
- Individual site (John Smith) – opinions about a motor car;
- Sports club – data on the team's performance;
- Government site – statistical information about the population of the country;
- Non-profit site – comments on particular law cases;
- Commercial company – the benefits of their products.

Discussion

In order to judge the quality of a site it is important to consider who is responsible for it, but, on its own, this is not sufficient for you to form an objective judgement.

Although it is important to know the author or organisation controlling the page, you will often need more information to judge quality. There are several other factors that can help with this:

* When was the material updated? Many subjects are very dynamic and rapidly become out-of-date. Most websites state when the page was last updated.
* Any statistical information needs to be accompanied by explanations of how it was collected (e.g. nature of sample, methods used and date collected).
* You should expect the same from a webpage author as you would of a conventional author of printed material (e.g. references, justification of conclusions, etc.).
* Material should be supported with references or links to other sites that contain quality information – explore the links.
* Is the same information available on a range of different sites? You can search for the same data on other sites and one positive indication is whether it features in directories (i.e. the editors have chosen it).
* The presentation of information can provide valuable clues to its quality (e.g. spelling and grammatical errors).
* Is the site well designed (e.g. does it provide assistance for using the site – site map, indexes, summaries and a help system).

Other resources
The internet is increasingly becoming the major way for students to locate information to help their studies. Many universities, colleges and other educational organisations are seeking to assist their learners by providing lists of useful websites. These are quality assured by the teaching staff and are therefore very useful. They are normally available within the organisation's intranet but in some cases are available on the organisation's website, meaning that, even if you are not a student of that institution, you can access the lists.

Many professional bodies also offer similar services to their members, usually directly related to the interest area of the institution. The Association of Computer Machinery (ACM), for example, offers its members the opportunity to access a digital library of papers relating to the use of computers. Many educational institutions offer access to their library catalogues so that you can identify books and other documents that might be useful. In most cases, however, these are not available in digital form and you would need to visit the library to use them. Some educational libraries allow students of recognised organisations to use their facilities, although usually you cannot borrow materials.

In recent years there has been a growth in online journals, some-

Activity   Judging quality

Using a search engine of your choice, try to locate information about one or more of the following topics:

1. First World War;
2. the first computer;
3. Australia.

Use the checklist below to assess the quality of the information presented in one or more pages.

QUALITY CHECKLIST

- Who is the author? Is biographical information provided?
- Who owns the site (e.g. consider the domain)? Are they appropriate for the information provided?
- Is it a personal site? Is it simply an individual's opinion?
- What references are incorporated within the information?
- What links are provided from the page? Are they good quality pages?
- When was the page last updated?
- Compare and contrast the different results.

Discussion

I located a quality site for information about Australia. It was the National Library of Australia – www.nla.gov.au. The indicators of quality are:

1. It is a national government site.
2. The site provides visitors with a detailed explanation of the site.
3. The pages are reviewed regularly, indicated by statements about when pages were last updated.
4. The site is governed by a service charter which is explained for users.
5. Users' privacy is protected by the site and this is explained by a privacy statement.
6. Feedback is encouraged in several ways, including email, telephone, fax and postal address details.
7. The site is linked to many other appropriate sites.
8. A search engine is provided to locate information within the site.
9. Help with using the site is provided.

The world wide web is dynamic, so that if you visit this site it is likely to have changed since my visit.

times linked to academic bodies and frequently having similar quality assurance procedures to the traditional print-based journals. These are sources of good quality information.

In some cases you can locate the email addresses of researchers working in your field to ask for advice. However, the growth of communication technologies has lead to a large increase in the use of email and many researchers receive hundreds of requests for information, making it difficult for help to be provided. If you need help from a researcher, email them with a short, modest, polite request explaining what you are seeking. However, you should have first explored the topic extensively to ensure that you cannot answer your question another way. A simple request is more likely to get a reply than a complex one. Some researchers have established websites to present information about their work and will simply direct you to consider their site, so seek it out before you email.

▶ Presenting information

ICT applications provide many useful ways of presenting information. For example:

- Microsoft Word is a modern word processing program that, in addition to helping you to write and present documents, will help you to create tables of information and to insert images into documents.
- Microsoft Excel is a modern spreadsheet program that lets you explore and model numerical data. In addition, it will allow you to present your numerical information in the form of charts and graphs.
- Digital cameras and scanners enable you to capture images and import them into your documents.

Tables
Using Microsoft Word, you can create tables of information. If you select the Table menu, and highlight the Insert option a pop up menu will be revealed. Click on the Table option to reveal the Insert Table window (Figure 3.13). This allows you to select the number of rows and columns that your table will contain.

Microsoft Word also provides many other functions to manipulate presentation of information in a table, including:

- inserting extra rows and columns;
- inserting extra cells;
- deleting rows and columns;
- deleting the whole table;
- fitting content of the table to its size;
- converting text into a table and a table into text;
- changing the thickness of the table lines using the Borders and Shading option within the Format menu;

Activity   Tables

Using Microsoft Word, create a table with three columns and ten rows. If you place your cursor on any of the table lines you will find that the cursor changes shape. If you hold down the left-hand mouse button, you can drag the column or row lines to narrow or widen them. Experiment with changing the table layout.

Discussion

Select the Table menu, highlight the Insert option to reveal a sub-menu and click on the Table item to display the Insert Table window. Enter 3 in the Number of columns and 10 in the Number of rows boxes, respectively then click on OK button. This will produce the table below:

The table below shows some changes that have been produced by dragging the row and column lines.

Figure 3.13   Inserting tables

- selecting table, row, column or cell;
- merging or splitting cells.

Charts and graphs

Microsoft Excel allows you to present your numerical information in the form of charts and graphs. Figure 3.14 illustrates a straightforward spreadsheet. Figures 3.15, 3.16, 3.17 and 3.18 illustrate different ways of presenting the data. There are several other ways of presenting information using Excel, for example as three-dimensional charts.

	Site A	Site B	Site C
Petrol	2300	3560	5320
Magazines	540	340	890
Food	230	410	750
Diesel	1230	1100	1450
Gas	670	530	875

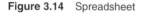

Figure 3.14   Spreadsheet

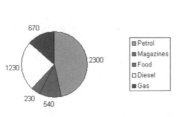

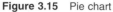

Figure 3.15   Pie chart

Activity   Manipulating tables

Using Microsoft Word, create a table with three columns and ten rows. Using the functions within Word, merge some cells, split some cells, delete two rows and make lines thicker.

Discussion

MERGE CELLS

Highlight two adjacent cells, select the Table menu and click on the Merge Cells. The chosen cells will now be merged into a single cell.

SPLIT CELLS

Place your cursor in the chosen cell, select the Table menu and click on the Split Cells. The chosen cell will now be split into two cells.

DELETE ROWS

Select the Table menu, highlight the Delete option and click on the Rows item. The row in which the cursor is placed will be removed.

THICKEN LINES

With the cursor within the table select the Table menu, highlight the Select option and click on the Table item. The whole table will be highlighted. Now select the Format menu and click on the Borders and Shading option to reveal the Borders and Shading window. Change the width of the line and click on OK button.

The table below shows the changes:

To use the chart features of Microsoft Excel input a spreadsheet into Excel. Highlight the parts of the sheet that you want to include in the chart or graph and then select the Insert menu and the Chart option to reveal the Chart Wizard – Step 1 to 4 – Chart Type window (Figure 3.19). You can select the type of chart and then adjust labels, axes and scales.

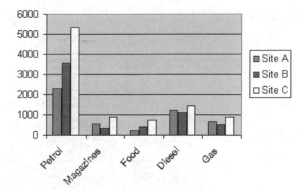

Figure 3.16 Histogram

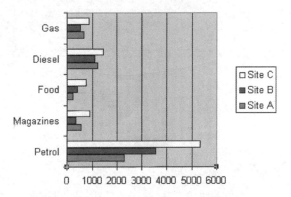

Figure 3.17 Bar chart

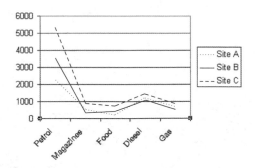

Figure 3.18 Line graph

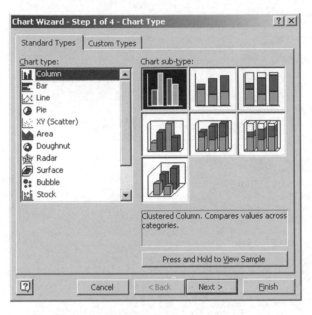

Figure 3.19 Chart Wizard

Activity   Charts and graphs

Create a 3-dimensional pie chart, column and line charts and graphs based on the spreadsheet below:

Table 3.2   Examination results

	Biology	Design and Technology	English	Mathematics	Science
Brown	45	52	56	49	60
Jones	67	71	69	67	74
Pascal	23	42	41	35	52
Rogers	43	49	53	42	56
Singh	67	75	68	82	84
Smith	56	63	64	71	42
Western	34	39	44	50	42

Discussion

My attempts are shown below: →

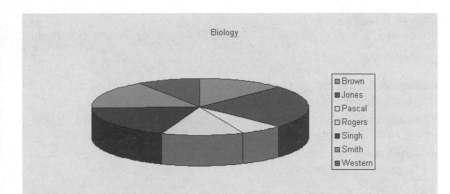

Biology

Figure 3.20   3-dimensional pie chart

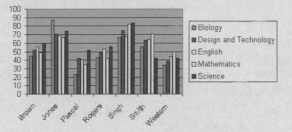

Figure 3.21   Column chart

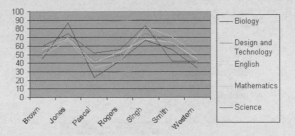

Figure 3.22   Line graph

These examples are provided to allow you to practise creating different types of charts, but in your own work you would need to decide what is the most appropriate way of presenting the information. In this case, which is the most effective way of comparing the data?

Digital images

There are a variety of ways of inserting images into a document, including:

- **digital cameras** – used to create a digital photograph which can be saved onto the computer and then inserted into your document;
- **scanners** – used to scan an image into the computer and in some cases directly into the application;
- **clip art** – these are collections of images supplied with applications or provided separately.

Microsoft Word provides functions to insert images from a camera or scanner as well as clip art and other pictures stored in a folder. You can also create a chart or insert one created in Excel. These functions are available by selecting the Insert menu and then highlighting the Picture option to reveal a sub-menu (Figure 3.23) that contains options for inserting pictures whether they are stored in a folder, Clip Art or from a camera or scanner.

If you select the Clip Art option then the Insert Clip Art window will appear to allow you to select an image. In some cases, you will see a message asking you to install the clip art option. This requires the use of the Microsoft Office CD-ROMs that will provide a step-by-step explanation of what you need to do.

If you select the From Scanner or Camera option, then the Insert Picture from Scanner or Camera window (Figure 3.24) appears. This allows you to identify the device you will be using and decide whether you want the image to be suitable for printing or for a website.

An alternative to importing an image into Word is to employ

Figure 3.23   Inserting images

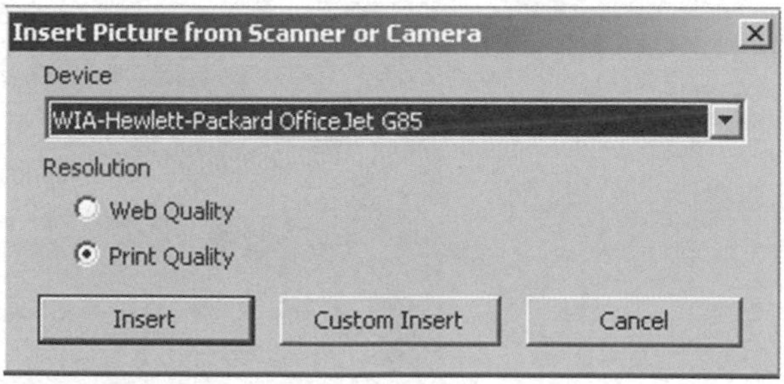

Insert Picture from Scanner or Camera   ☒

Device

WIA-Hewlett-Packard OfficeJet G85   ▼

Resolution

    ○ Web Quality

    ⦿ Print Quality

    [Insert]   [Custom Insert]   [Cancel]

Figure 3.24   Insert Image from Scanner

Activity   Picture

Using a scanner or digital camera, import a picture into a document using either Microsoft Word or Windows Paint applications.

Discussion

The image in Figure 3.25 was scanned into the document.

Figure 3.25   Imported figure

Windows Paint. This program will scan or import pictures from a digital camera and you can then crop the image using the Paint functions.

Creating an image

You can create images yourself using a variety of tools, but Microsoft Windows includes an application within the Accessories menu called Paint (see Figure 3.26).

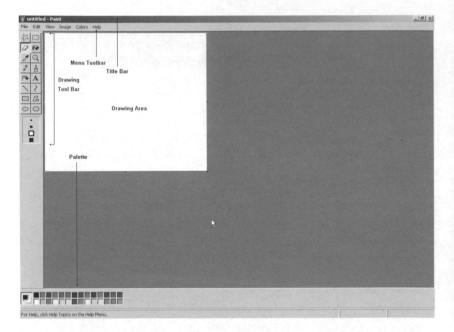

Figure 3.26 Windows Paint

Activity   Drawing

Using Windows Paint or another drawing application, create a drawing using the standard drawing tools.

Discussion

My effort can be seen in Figure 3.27. I used the rectangle, circle, eclipse, polygon, fill and paint brush.

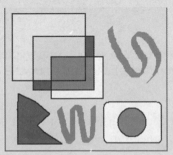

Figure 3.27

►Copyright

It is important to realise that information published on the world wide web is covered by copyright in the same way as traditional forms of publications. It is, therefore, critical to check the conditions placed on the online content. Frequently, this is available on the home page. You will sometimes need to look at the bottom of the page where, in small type, you will see statements about copyright terms and conditions. In other cases, sites will clearly indicate if you can copy the material.

In all cases, you must assume that the material is copyrighted. This does not mean that in all circumstances you cannot copy the material. You can do so under the Fair Dealings Provision, which allows individuals to copy content for personal research, study, criticism and review. However, you must only copy those parts which are essential for the purpose and you must acknowledge the source and copyright holder. This does not apply to music, video and sheet music.

Many colleges, training centres and other educational institutions provide their students with guidance about copyright and you should seek the advice of your tutor and institution.

►Plagiarism

The world wide web provides you with access to a huge resource of information. It is very easy to copy this work. However, to represent as your own work the efforts of other people (plagiarism) is a serious offence which, if discovered, may lead to you failing your course. Many colleges will be able to provide you with guidance on how to quote the work of writers without plagiarising them. It is a part of academic writing to quote from the work of other people, but it is essential that it is clearly identified by enclosing it in quotation marks, identifying the source in the text (e.g. 'Clarke 2001') or by some other acceptable means. Your college will provide specific guidance.

There now exists a number of electronic methods to identify plagiarism so it is probably easier now to detect cheating than at any other time.

▶ Utilities

Often, when you are accessing online resources, you will need utility programmes called Plug-ins. They extend the capabilities of the browser, allowing you to hear audio files, see videos, experience animation, etc. Plug-ins are normally freely available and, when you access a resource that requires one, they will offer you the opportunity to download the utility. Some examples of plug-ins are:

- Apple QuickTime
- RealPlayer
- Macromedia Flash

Some employer and college networks will not allow you to download files as a measure to prevent virus infection. However, if they are providing e-learning opportunities, they will also provide all the plug-ins and utilities you need.

▶ Summary

1. **Assessing your skills**
   You need a range of information and communication technology skills in order to be an effective e-learner. It is important to assess the level and range of your skills and to develop a personal programme to continually improve them.

2. **Accessibility**
   Within Microsoft Windows operating system, there are a range of options to help you make the system more accessible. These include changing the contrast of the display, removing the need to press multiple keys, allowing you to make errors with key presses, adding sound effects, displaying messages when the system uses sound, making the mouse suitable for left-handed users and using the keyboard as an alternative to the mouse.

3. **File management**
   It is important to establish an efficient and effective filing system. The key is to make file and folder names meaningful and to create a clear structure.

Microsoft Windows provides you with many functions within Windows Explorer. These include:

- creating a new folder;
- deleting a file or folder;
- renaming a file or folder;
- cutting, copying and pasting files and folders;
- dragging and dropping files and folders.

4. File formats

Computer information is stored as a file. Files are given extensions (e.g. .doc) to their names depending on the type of data they contain and an icon is added to assist with identification.

5. Applications

When you buy an application, it is governed by a licence. This controls your use of the application (e.g. limiting the number of copies of the software that you can use simultaneously). It is important to read the licence which is included in the packaging or displayed during the installation process.

In addition to commercial software products, there are:

- shareware products that allow you to test them before purchase;
- freeware applications that are free

The degree of technical support varies considerably between commercial, shareware and freeware products. Before you buy any product it is important to check the system requirements for the product (e.g. type of processor and memory).

6. Compressing files

There are several ways of transferring files between computer systems. These include:

- saving the files to a floppy disc;
- sending the file as an email attachment – some email systems limit the size of the attachments they will accept;
- saving large files to a CD-RW disc;
- saving large files to a USB dongle.

There are several ways of reducing the size of files. These include:

- compressing the file using a specialist application (e.g. Winzip);
- changing the format of the picture, although this may reduce the quality of image files.

It is good and essential practice to virus check all files that you receive from any source and also those files that you transfer to other systems.

7. **Tracking changes**
   Microsoft Word provides you with a Track Changes function that lets you see all the changes that have been made to a document. You can then choose to accept or reject each change.

8. **Saving and backing up your information**
   It is essential to:

   - save your work regularly (i.e. every few minutes);
   - back up all your files regularly;
   - assess how often you need to copy all your information to a transferable medium.

9. **Searching the world wide web**
   Two vital skills for using the world wide web are locating information and judging its quality. To help you find information there are specialist sites called search engines, which fall into three main categories:

   - individual – searches a database it has created of webpages;
   - meta – searches several databases created by other search engines;
   - directory – searches a list of sites compiled by the staff of the search engine.

   You can search for a variety of resources including:

   - webpages;
   - images;
   - discussion groups;
   - news;
   - individual email addresses.

Keywords

All search engines require you to locate information by entering keywords. Each one operates differently, so you need to learn how your chosen engine works. Some tips are:

- explore what happens with different words;
- be direct;
- read search engine feedback and act on it;
- signs will change how your words are matched with webpages (e.g. a plus sign ensures that all the words you enter are present on the matched pages; inverted commas match the exact phrase; the minus symbol eliminates pages containing the information; you can also combine symbols). However, each search engine will treat symbols in a different way.

Boolean

Another way of searching is to use Boolean logic. There are three operators:

- OR (i.e. Napoleon OR Wellington – locate pages with the words Napolean or Wellington);
- AND (i e. Napoleon AND Wellington – locate pages with both the words Napoleon and Wellington);
- NOT (i.e. Napoleon NOT Wellington – locate pages with the words Napoleon but not Wellington).

Favorites

A browser provides you with the means of recording the addresses of important webpages so that you can easily locate them again. In Internet Explorer you use the Favorites function and in Netscape the same function is called Bookmarking.

10. Assessing the quality of online information

It is essential that you become able to assess the quality of information presented on the world wide web, not least because anyone can develop a site. Some ways of assessing quality include:

- Who produced the site – are they appropriate to the information it displays?

- Does it display personal views?
- Can you contact the site to ask about the content?
- When was the site material last updated?
- Does the site explain how the information was collected (e.g. samples)?
- Is the information justified (e.g. references to other published sources)?
- What links to other sites are presented?
- Is the information presented available on a range of other sites?
- How well presented is the information?
- How well designed is the site?

11. Presenting information (tables, charts and graphs)

You will often need to present information effectively as part of your studies. Computer applications provide various ways of displaying information, for example:

- Microsoft Word helps you to create and manipulate tables of information;
- Microsoft Excel allows you to present numerical information in a wide range of forms.

12. Digital images

There are numerous ways of importing images into a document:

- digital cameras;
- scanners;
- clip art.

You can also create your own images using painting and drawing applications (e.g. Windows Paint).

13. Copyright

All content published on the world wide web is covered by copyright in the same way as a printed document. You must check the conditions for its use before you copy any information. Conditions are often displayed on the home page.

14. Plagiarism

It is easy to copy information using a computer but representing the work of others as your own (plagiarism) is a serious offence. You may fail your course if you are discovered plagiarising other people's work.

15. Utilities

Plug-ins are utility programmes that extend the capability of your browser to access audio, video, animation or other resources.

4 Learning Environments

e-Learning can take many forms and is often linked to the environment in which the course or programme is based. This chapter will concentrate on developing an understanding of the nature of the e-learning environments and approaches including:

- synchronous learning (e.g. text, audio or video conferencing);
- managed learning environments (Course Management Systems);
- Virtual Learning Environment (Learning Management Systems);
- world wide web;
- intranets/extranets;
- groupware;
- WebQuests;
- blended learning;

The chapter will discuss how these different environments provide support for learners and what learners can expect from the e-learning course in terms of peer support/communication, tutor support/ communication, moderation of online communication and assessment. There is also a physical component of e-learning, in that you need to access a computer and communication system. There are several choices of location and you may well use more than one. The main choices are a learning centre, cybercafe, mobile equipment, your home and your workplace.

▶ Places to learn

Learning centre
Although a learning centre is not an online environment, it is often the physical location where you can access the e-learning resources. Many colleges, training facilities and community sites have developed learning or ICT centres to provide individuals with access to computer and

communication technology. In colleges they are often in or closely associated with the library, while private companies may link them to a collection of learning resources. College centres can be very large with hundreds of computers, whereas community sites may contain only two or three. Thus, there can be large differences in size, range of facilities and environment between different centres.

A college learning centre may well encourage the establishment of a quiet structured climate in which to study and most college centres will provide you with technical and learning support. Using a public facility is different from studying in your own room and requires different preparation. In large centres, the comings and goings of other people can be distracting. If you feel you need a more disciplined environment, then a college centre may be a good choice. You also frequently gain the benefit of a high speed link to the internet.

The limitations are that you probably need to book a terminal and your use will be limited by the centre's policy on, for example, how long you can use the terminal. However, many colleges are now opening centres 24 hours a day for 365 days a year, so if you want to study in the middle of the night you can. Although college centres are usually free for registered students, they will often charge for extra services such as colour printing and photocopying. You may not be allowed to bring information from home on a floppy disk or CD-ROM as a precaution against the transmission of viruses.

Cybercafe

Many cybercafes have been opened across the world, so that when you are away from home or college you can carry on with your studies. Cybercafes and associated public access take a variety of forms. Internet kiosks are often found at airports, railway stations and other public transport sites. Cybercafes can be found in many holiday resorts, including on some cruise ships. The cost and nature of using this type of service will vary, but the cost can limit the length of time you can spend online. You may also need to pay extra for printing or downloading information.

Mobile

Portable computer equipment (e.g. laptop and notebook computers and PDAs), combined with mobile phone or wireless technology can allow you to connect to the internet almost anywhere. This provides the possibility of learning while you are away from home or work or even while you are travelling. Many people travel as part of their work, so learning on a train or at an airport is possible.

Although portable equipment has become lighter and easier to trans-port it still needs to be carried and although portable printers are available their use is probably limited to hotel rooms rather than on a train. Nevertheless you need more than access to the online resources to learn. You also want an environment that helps you learn. A busy and noisy waiting room or a crowded train are not ideal.

Home
In your own room you have ready access to all your materials, books and other resources, whereas when you visit a public resource you need to take everything with you. You are free to employ your personal computer in any way you want, whereas a public/college resource will require you to comply with its condition. Your freedom is therefore maximised at home, but, in order to benefit fully, you will need self-discipline. Learning normally requires a quiet and distraction-free environment. If you share your home with other students or your family, it is likely that at some times it is noisy and full of people.

To be a successful home-based online learner, you must create a suitable learning environment. This is not simply a physical space, although you do need to be organised with your books, papers and other learning tools to hand. The learning environment includes the understanding of the people who share your home so that they will help you learn by providing you with peace and space. Family and friends are very important learning supporters and their understanding will help if things get difficult.

Workplace
Many people now work with a computer linked to the internet as a normal tool of their employment, so the workplace may be a suitable place to undertake e-learning. This is a familiar place and you will have some freedom to customise the environment to meet your needs. You will probably have access to a fast connection to the internet as well as printers and technical support. However, many workplaces are open plan with limited privacy. Telephones and colleagues are likely to interrupt your studies and it is not always easy to achieve a long quiet period.

Many employers provide learning centres, since they feel the work-station is unsuitable for long periods of studying. However, the concept of learning in small chunks (e.g. 15 to 30 minutes) is well established and this is probably suitable for workplace learning even in noisy environments. Another approach is to divert your telephone, put on

Activity   Learning location

Consider your own needs and approach to learning and which learning environments would be best for you.

Discussion

It is likely that all the options will have attractive features and also negative aspects. No one of them is likely to be perfect for everyone. People have dfferent preferences. Some like complete quiet, while others prefer some background music; some people are able to concentrate even in noisy environments and some even find noise an aid to concentrating. There is no one ideal place for e-learning for everyone. Many learners use several locations such as home, college and work.

earphones and put up a sign asking not to be disturbed. This may give you a relatively quiet and distraction free area for a long enough period.

Obviously, if you do not work at a desk or have the freedom to ask for uninterrupted time, then your workplace is unsuitable. Managers are familiar with staff being given time off to attend a class, but may find it difficult to adjust when you do not leave but you are studying and therefore unavailable. It is sensible when you are seeking agreement to undertake an e-learning course to explain to your manager that there will be times when you cannot be disturbed. It is sensible to agree a pattern, so that your manager and colleagues know you are studying. However, even if you agree everything and have a supportive manager, you are more likely to be disturbed since, in the workplace, the work is always likely to be given priority over your studies. Table 4.1 compares and contrasts the five locations we have discussed for e-learning access.

▶ Synchronous learning (e.g. text, audio or video conferencing)

A great deal of emphasis is placed in e-learning on asynchronous methods (e.g. email) but text, video and audio conferencing are also part of e-learning and they are all synchronous (that is, you use them at the same time as the other students and the tutor). The technology for text, audio and video conference varies. It can mean interacting with other learners through a large screen with high quality images and sound or through a computer display where only a small image of

Table 4.1   Comparison of learning environments

Environment	Strengths	Weaknesses
Learning centre	1. Fast broadband connection 2. Technical support 3. Learning support 4. Structured learning environment 5. Access to peripherals (e.g. colour printers, scanners, etc.)	1. Need to book time 2. May be visually distracting due to size 3. Charge for colour printing and other services 4. Restrict or prevent the use of your own disks and data from home
Cybercafe	1. Many locations throughout the world 2. Informal and easy to use 3. Sometimes will have a fast connection to the internet	1. Are sometimes expensive 2. Restrict or prevent the use of your own disks and data from home 3. Charge extra for colour printing and other services
Mobile	1. Learn wherever you want and need to 2. Maximise the time you have available	1. Need to own or have access to portable computer and mobile phone or similar technology 2. Equipment has to be carried 3. Limited peripherals available when travelling 4. Limited speed of access to the internet ➔

your peers and tutor can be seen. In some cases, you can only see a still image of the students combined with their voices, or even sound only.

The concept behind text conferencing is simple and perhaps because of this it is probably the most used form of synchronous conferencing. You can send a message which everyone else logged onto the system can see and respond to. However, text conferencing systems vary considerably so that what appears on the screen can, to a large extent, be different from application to application. The original systems simply presented the messages, one after another, in the order that they arrived at the computer. Later in this chapter, we will consider threaded discussions in an asynchronous email group. Threads are a way of presenting separate elements of a discussion so you can more easily follow its flow. Synchronous text conferencing can also be presented as threads (i.e. each part of the debate identified). Messages

Table 4.1 Comparison of learning environments – *continued*

Environment	Strengths	Weaknesses
		5. Unstructured and distracting learning environment
Home	1. Freedom to learn in the way you prefer (e.g. during the night) 2. Personal learning resources readily available	1. Limited range of equipment available at home 2. Speed of access to the internet may be limited 3. Unstructured learning environment 4. Potentially noisy and distracting at times
Workplace	1. Fast broadband connection 2. Technical support 3. Familiar place 4. Integrate learning with your work 5. Access to printers and other peripherals	1. Possibly a noisy and distracting environment (e.g. telephones) 2. In some cases a stressful environment 3. Needs a desk-based job with some freedom 4. Need to agree study time with manager and colleagues 5. Work always likely to take priority over learning

to text conferences are stored so that you can trace ideas and discuss them later.

There are several ways of organising conferencing including:

- students being placed together in a classroom with the tutor linked to them through text, video or audio conferencing;
- several groups of students in different locations interacting with a remote tutor;
- individual students at many different locations interacting with a tutor at the educational institute.

In some of these scenarios, the experience is broadly similar to listening to a lecture and, in fact, video conferencing has frequently been used to provide a lecture from an expert to thousands of people simultaneously. This is highly efficient in that many can see and hear the lecture, but the opportunity to question the speaker is poor, and it is very similar to listening to a lecture in a large hall. In this situation, the learner should treat it as a lecture and take notes.

In some cases, the lecture will be recorded and you can review the material later on your own or with other learners. It is often more effective to watch video material with others so that you can discuss it. This can give you a better insight into the content than simply working on your own.

Let us consider the e-learning skills required when you are taking part individually, with other students based in different locations. In most cases, interaction will be through a computer screen with relatively low quality images, but probably reasonable sound. The closest traditional method to this scenario is a tutorial or seminar where you can interact directly with your peers. The difference is that in a face-to-face situation you can easily judge when to make a contribution. This is quite difficult during video conferencing, since you are likely to only see one image at a time or, if there are many images, the size will be so small that details are unclear. The tutor's role is to ensure that everyone has an opportunity to contribute and this can make the procedure a little mechanical and slow, since you have to wait for your turn to speak.

Audio conferencing is very similar to a telephone conference call with a group of people seated around a conference telephone. It is possible to have a pure audio conference or audio with still images. The tutor can send you images or documents as part of the system or as email attachments.

Synchronous learning is broadly similar to traditional classroom approaches. If you are taking part as a group of students, both video and audio require you to take notes to fully benefit from the experience. A new opportunity is created if students are working together as the possibility of asking questions is maximised. With audio conferencing, you may be able to confer with the other learners during the conference away from the microphones. Table 4.2 gives an overview of the learning skills and strategies that may be beneficial in conferencing situations.

Synchronous text conferencing can be used for a wide range of purposes, such as expert discussion and tutorials. A tutor may publish a paper on a course topic to all the students and invite questions, views and ideas arising from reading it. The messages can be archived to form a type of annotation to the paper. Some institutions employ text conferencing to provide additional student help by ensuring a tutor is

Table 4.2 Text, video and audio conferencing

Structure	Text conferencing	Video conferencing	Audio conferencing
Learners are together, but separated from the tutor	1. This is not a common model for text conferencing and you will rarely encounter it	1. Note taking is important 2. Discuss and organise with your colleagues to gain the maximum benefit 3. View recording later to complete notes or clarify any confusion 4. Regard event as a lecture or seminar	1. Note taking is important 2. Discuss and organise with your colleagues to gain the maximum benefit 3. Opportunity to discuss with peers during conference away from the communication technology
Learners and tutor all at different locations	1. Text conferencing tends to be more spontaneous than other synchronous methods but useful to have identified questions, concerns and ideas in advance 2. Record of discussion is normally stored by the system 3. Concentration is less important since all messages appear on the screen and you can catch up if interrupted, but best practice is to focus on the communications without interruptions	1. Prepare your contribution and questions in advance 2. Note taking is important, including recording other learners' comments 3. Concentration is critical so ensure you are not interrupted	1. Prepare your contribution and questions in advance 2. Note taking is important, including recording other learners' comments 3. Concentration is critical, so ensure you are not interrupted

available between set times to answer any questions arising from the course. Students can ask their question and the tutor will answer immediately. Other students can join in if they wish, but normally there is no compulsion to take part. This is similar to a tutor being physically available on a Wednesday afternoon in classroom three to provide extra help to anyone who chooses to attend. Text conferencing allows the limitations of a set location to be eliminated.

► Groupware

'Groupware' is the term for applications that allow people linked through a network (e.g. internet) to share information and work co-operatively and collaboratively. It is possible with groupware to work with others to share an application (e.g. whiteboard) as part of a synchronous group project. The application sharing is usually combined with an audio conference or real-time text communication. The group may be seeking to design a product, investigate a concept or work on one of many other possibilities. Group working is only suitable for small groups of learners (i.e. 4 to 6) and requires that everyone is a competent user of the shared application and communication system. A successful group activity requires that:

- the objectives of the exercise are agreed and limited;
- a time limit has been agreed (i.e. more time is normally needed online than for a similar task face-to-face);
- a structure has been agreed so that everyone has an equal opportunity to contribute;
- each learner has a role within the team (e.g. note taker, spokesperson, etc.) although in some cases the initial task is to agree roles for each participant;
- there has been good preparation so that the effectiveness of online time is maximised.

► Managed Learning Environment (MLE) or Course Management System (CMS)

A Managed Learning Environment (MLE) or Course Management System (CMS) refers to the integration of a variety of software systems that form the overall online administration and learning environment for the institution. There is a variety of commercial MLE products available and many educational organisations have developed their own structures and processes. This means that there is no single definition of all the elements that are contained within an MLE. However, an MLE is likely to provide:

- An administration system that tracks learners' achievement and maintains a record of their progress and achievements.
- Financial, attendance and registration records.
- Course information about all the learning opportunities available.
- Learning resources:
  - interactive learning materials,
  - learning resources (e.g. guides, examples and self-assessment tests),
  - links to off-line resources.
- Library catalogues and loan system.
- Quality Assurance systems.
- Communication systems:
  - email;
  - conferencing;
  - chatrooms;
  - bulletin boards.
- An assessment system (e.g. records of test results and in some cases the actual online assessments; in many cases testing involves both online and offline methods).
- Support systems (e.g. tutors, mentors and peers).
- Advice (e.g. finance, childcare, health and careers).
- Information (e.g. health and safety, equal opportunities and policies).
- Online courses.

▶ Virtual Learning Environment (VLE) or Learning Management System (LMS)

A Virtual Learning Environment (VLE) or Learning Management System (LMS) essentially refers to the elements of the MLE that are intended to support and deliver the online learning. The systems can be called by either name or neither. In some cases a VLE stands alone. There is no universal definition of what a VLE contains, so each institution may offer a different environment. Some institutions have devel-

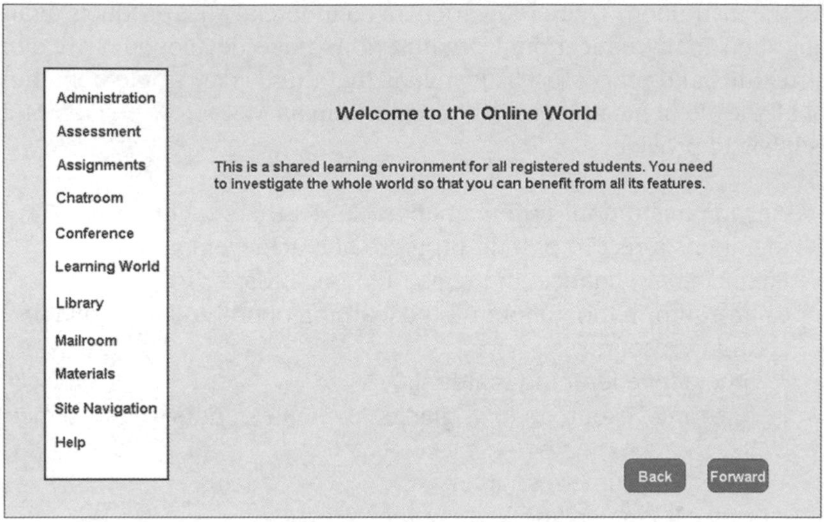

Figure 4.1   Example of a Virtual Learning Environment

oped their own system and called themselves a Virtual College or other
locally derived name. Figure 4.1 shows an example of the home page
of a Virtual Learning Environment. The list of links down the left-hand
side of the page shows the range of facilities and functions that you
might expect to find in an MLE/VLE. Figure 4.2 illustrates an online

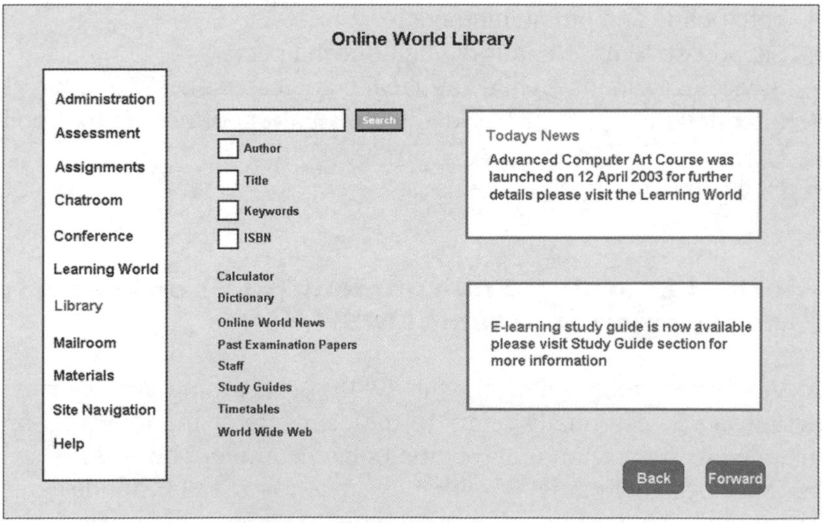

Figure 4.2   Example of a Virtual Learning Environment library

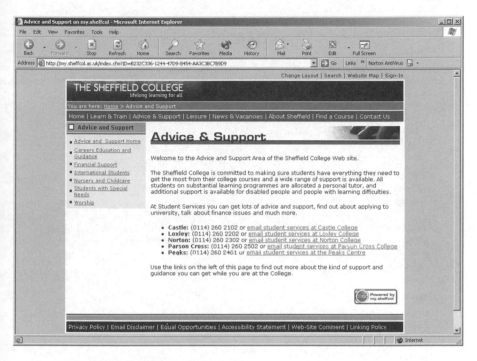

Figure 4.3   Sheffield College website

library with a search facility to help you locate books or other resources. A list of popular facilities is often included to enable rapid access to them. News items are sometimes displayed in various parts of the environment to draw your attention to new developments.

Many institutions provide similar facilities and functions to those co-ordinated and managed within a MLE/VLE. In some case these are signposted within the institution's website or intranet. Figure 4.3 shows a webpage from the Sheffield College website.

For many institutions, the introduction of an MLE/VLE requires significant organisational change in that it represents a major difference in the way the organisation operates.

▶ World wide web

The world wide web is a vast resource for any learner studying almost any subject. There are many sites that can be helpful to you including:

Activity   Managed Learning Environments/Virtual Learning Environments – A

If you are a learner in a college or other education or training institution that does not provide an MLE/VLE then:

1. Search the world wide web – Managed Learning Environment and Course Management System. Some suppliers are Blackboard, WebCT, COSE, Fretwell Downing, Futuremedia Solstra and TekniCAL Virtual Campus. You might also visit the FERL Becta website which has research and information about VLEs (http://ferl.becta.org.uk).
2. Search the world wide web – Virtual Learning Environment and Learning Management System.

You should locate a range of webpages that refer to both MLEs and VLEs. Some sites will offer to demonstrate them. Take part in one of the demonstrations which will help you gain an appreciation of the nature of the environment and what functions/facilities are provided.

Discussion

You should notice that the names of MLE and VLE vary across different products and that a range of commercial and college systems are available. Facilities and functions will differ, but will have a core of broadly similar aims and objectives (e.g. to aid collaborative learning).

Activity   Managed Learning Environments/Virtual Learning Environments – B

If you are a registered learner in a college or other education or training institution that does provide a MLE/VLE then:

1. Systematically explore the environment and make notes of each facility that you might want to use during your course.
2. You may find the environment has virtual guided tours to help you understand how to use the MLE/VLE, so take part in one.

Discussion

You should find many useful features that will help you with your learning. In many cases, there are detailed elements that are helpful, such as other learners' lists of useful publications, access to past examination papers and examples of assignments. It is essential that you become a competent user of the MLE, since it can provide you with an enormous amount of support.

- biography;
- libraries and book shops;
- dictionary;
- electronic journals;
- online databases.

The world wide web is essentially a huge information library. It is important when using information from the world wide web to reference the source. Most colleges will now include guidance on the format of online citations.

Example:

- Clarke, A. (2004), e-Learning Skills, www.justanexample.net, accessed on 26 May 2004.

Biographies
There is a wide variety of web sites concerned with biographical information about famous people. The activity below provides you with the opportunity to locate biographical sources.

Activity   Biography

Using a search engine of your choice to try to locate information about Winston Churchill that relates to his childhood.

Try using one of the specialist biographical resources below:

- www.biography.com/ – many thousands of biographies
- www.s9.com/biography/ – biographical dictionary
- http://amillionlives.com/ – links to many biographical resources
- www.anb.org/ – American National Biography

Discussion
By entering Winston Churchill, my search using the Google search engine located 441 000 pages. A further search within these results adding the word childhood reduced the number of hits to 21 000 and when Harrow (the name of his school) was added, 655 pages were listed.
   Now try to locate information about someone else.

Libraries and book shops

Books are probably the major learning resource for any student. Your tutors will often provide you with reading lists of articles, books and journals that you should study. The major practical issue is to locate the books and other resources. It is now common practice for college libraries and learning centres to have their catalogues available electronically. The library databases are available for you to search. Some catalogues will tell you if the book is available or if it has been borrowed by another student, where the book is physically situated and the length of time you can borrow it. Some colleges have placed their catalogues online, so you can carry out your search from your home or local centre without the need to travel. In addition to the college library, there are also online libraries.

You may also seek to buy books. The world wide web is rich in online book shops that often have an enormous range of stock and, in some cases, they are linked to second-hand book shops enabling you to find used or out-of-print titles.

Activity   Books

Using a search engine of your choice, search for Online Book Shops. Once you have located a list of online shops, select one and investigate what services it provides.

Discussion

My search on Google identified 1 250 000 hits. I browsed the first few pages of hits and found a wide range of shops as well as some pages that gave reviews of online book shops.

I chose to visit Amazon (www.amazon.com) and found that:

1. The site provided a range of goods including books – both new and used – computer hardware and software, music and videos.
2. You could search for books by simply entering the author's name, title or keyword and a list of possible matches was provided.
3. Books were described (e.g. length, cost and publisher) and in some cases there were examples of the book's content.
4. In some cases, the book had been reviewed by readers and occasionally the author had provided some comments.
5. You could buy the book immediately using a credit card.

I found the experience broadly similar to browsing the titles in a high street book shop.

Activity   Library

Visit the Internet Public Library (www.ipl.org/ – Internet Public Library) and explore the resource. Follow some of the links and investigate what is available.

Discussion

Your own experience is likely to be different, owing to the dynamic nature of the world wide web, but I noticed three different features of the home page:

* reference items (e.g. encyclopaedia and quotations);
* reading room;
* subject collection.

When I linked to both the encyclopaedia and quotations items, I was taken to a list of online resources that related to them. I found a site that would help me to identify suitable quotations.

The reading room gave me access to a search facility and when I entered the word 'Learning' I located 34 matches. When I followed one of the matches, I was able to read the publication online and find out how to buy it.

I clicked on the education subject collection and was presented with a list of sub-headings from which I chose adult education. This linked me to a list of websites related to adult education and by following the links I discovered the Canadian Office of Learning Technology site and their publications, which I could download or print in some cases.

What did you discover?

Dictionaries

Dictionaries are useful for all learners and they can be located on the world wide web at sites such as:

* http://dictionary.reference.com/
* www.askoxford.com/

Electronic journals (e-journals, webjournals or online journals)

There has recently been a large growth in the number of electronic journals covering a wide range of topics. They are sometimes electronic versions of conventional paper journals, but many are only available in electronic form. Some you can only get through subscription, but many are free. e-Journals vary in presentation as much as conventional ones do. Some offer access to an archive of past editions and so provide a rich resource (e.g. http://scholar.lib.vt.edu/ejournals/JTE/ – Journal of Technology Education).

Activity   Dictionary

Visit http://dictionary.reference.com/, www.askoxford.com/ and any other dictionary sites. Compare the sites by seeking definitions for:

- serendipity;
- palliative;
- dendritic;
- reflex.

Discussion

I was unable to find definitions for all four words. How did you do?

Many journals allow students to download or print a copy of articles, but you should check the conditions under which this facility is provided.

Online databases

Many websites provide users with databases of useful information. There are two main types:

- full-text;
- bibliographic.

Full-text databases provide you with a copy of a whole entry, often in the form of articles from online or conventional journals or research papers. Bibliographic databases hold the details of a publication with a short summary of its contents. This allows you to locate the item through a library or book shop. Both types of database are often provided by college or national library services, while access to some is by subscription. That said, many colleges are subscribers, so check which ones your college has linked to.

Downloading

The world wide web offers a variety of opportunities to download files containing documents or other resources. The process is straightforward – normally you only have to doubleclick on the downloadable file on a website to start the process. Your operating system will ask you where you want to save the file to or if you want to open it. Figure 4.4 illustrates the Save As window. You should select which folder to save the file into and change the file's name to one which is meaningful to

Activity   e-Journal

Using the search engine of your choice, locate a range of journals. Access two or three, then compare and contrast them. Investigate:

* access to contents;
* how you subscribe;
* notification;
* conditions for downloading and printing;
* conditions for authors;
* search facilities;
* links.

Discussion

You should find that access to content varies depending on whether the journal is free or only available on subscription. Sometimes, you only have access to abstracts or sample articles rather than the whole text, but in many cases you can view the whole journal.

Subscription to online journals is usually by email and will, in some cases, require a fee to be paid. Most will notify you by email that a new edition is available so you can visit the website.

Most journals require you to adhere to their conditions for accessing, downloading or printing content (e.g. the copy is for personal use and the source must be acknowledged).

Many provide detailed guidance for prospective authors, which can be useful for readers in that it provides evidence on which to judge the quality and objectivity of the papers (e.g. all submissions will be reviewed by three independent members of the editorial committee).

Some journals allow you access to previous editions and occasionally in some cases there is a search engine to help you locate papers relating to a particular subject.

Many journal sites offer links to other related websites. Indeed, e-Journals are a very useful resource.

If you are a registered student at an educational institution, you will find that many subscription journals are available to you as part of your course and you will be given passwords to enable you to access them.

you. When you have a large number of files it is easy to forget a name or a location so try always to use memorable names.

Downloading is straightforward, but should never be attempted unless you are confident that your virus protection software is up-to-date and that the site you are downloading from is likely to take precautions against virus infection.

In order to read a file, you must have the application that created it or a compatible one on your system.

Activity   Investigate Online Databases and Resources

ERIC – Educational Resource Information Center (http://eric.ed.gov/) – is a major online resource containing a bibliographical database.
   Visit the site and explore the possibilities offered by the resource. In particular:

1. Consider what help is provided– explore all the links.
2. Use the internal search engine to investigate the database – try searching using the different options and see the results of searching for 'learning skills' and then varying the types of publications included using the advanced search options (e.g. doctoral dissertations, books, etc.) and other optional characteristics.
3. Find a publication relevant to your course.
4. Consider the advantages and limitations of using the ERIC resources.

Continue until you are confident that you can use the resource.

Discussion

1. While searching a resource such as ERIC you will notice that you need to use the site's own search engine in a similar way to the way you would to locate information on the world wide web. If you search for learning skills without any qualifying criteria you will locate the maximum number of hits, whereas adding a few optional criteria will limit the results to a more manageable total.
2. You will have noticed that you can purchase copies of some of the documents.

Online databases are important resources.

Reading online documents

There are already many e-books and other electronic documents available on the world wide web and intranets. In order to read these publications, you often need the use of specific reader applications, usually freely available from their producers. Two major suppliers of e-book applications are Adobe and Microsoft, which both provide free reading applications providing you agree to abide by their licence agreements.

Frequently asked questions

Many websites include a section called 'frequently asked questions' (FAQs). These attempt to identify the questions that visitors to the site will be likely to ask and to provide model answers for them. They are often a valuable asset, because you can quickly locate the information you are seeking during your visit to the site.

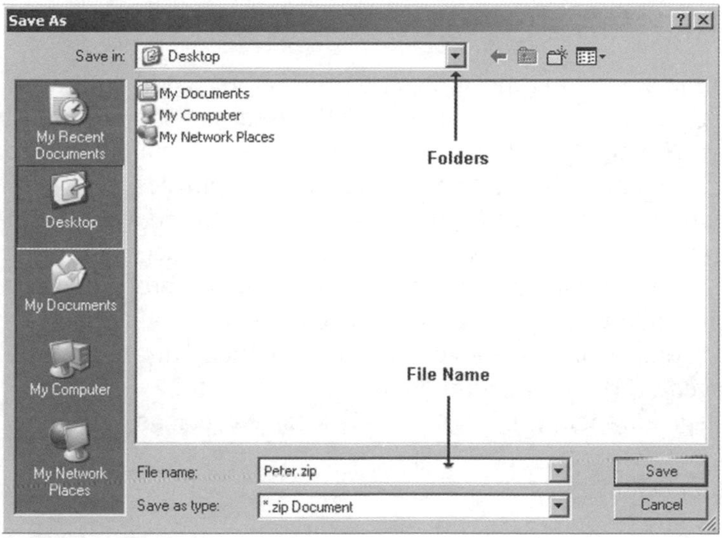

Figure 4.4   Downloading a file – Save As window (Windows XP)

Actlvlty   Adobe Acrobat and Microsoft readers

You are able to download Adobe Acrobat and Microsoft readers from

• www.adobe.com/support/downloads/main.html and
• www.microsoft.com/reader/default.asp

Visit these sites and read the licence agreements which govern the use of the products and then, if you are able to agree to the conditions, download and install the readers on your computer.
   Now search the world wide web until you locate free e-books or other documents in both Adobe and Microsoft formats and try to open them. You should find that if you have the readers installed on your computer they will open automatically.
   Explore the facilities available within the readers.

Discussion

There are a variety of opportunities to download resources from the world wide web. However, their use is controlled by their licence agreements, so you should always read the agreement before downloading the material since by downloading it you are accepting its terms.
   The two readers operate in different ways so compare and contrast them.

▶ Intranets/extranets

An intranet is an organisation's own miniature world wide web. It is normally a private area that only authorised persons are allowed to access. A majority of large companies and many small and medium sized ones have created intranets for their employees. Many colleges have also built intranets for their students, so that many of their facilities can have an online presence. Students can access the intranet from a college computer or from home, usually through the college website and by using a user identification (User ID) code and a password. Some colleges and employers call their intranets portals or Managed Learning Environments.

College intranets will often provide facilities such as:

- library catalogues;
- learning resources;
- administration;
- careers advice;
- assessment records;
- course details;
- course timetables.

Extranets are a variation between the complete open access of the internet and the closed world of an intranet. An extranet is designed to be an intranet that is open to outside users through the use of a password and an agreed user identification. They are often used to facili-

---

Activity   Intranet

If you are a learner in a college or other education/training institution that provides an intranet:

1. Systematically explore the intranet environment and make a note of each facility that you might want to use during your course.
2. You may find that there is a help facility, an introduction to the intranet or other form of assistance available.

Discussion

You should find many useful features that will help you with your learning. Often there are detailed elements such as other learners' lists of useful publications, access to past examination papers and examples of assignments. It is essential that you become a competent user of the intranet.

tate group work so that individuals who are geographically spread out can co-operate on a joint project.

▶ WebQuests

WebQuests were developed at San Diego State University (Dodge and March, 1995). They are, as the name suggests, about undertaking a task using the information available on the world wide web to achieve a set objective. They can take a variety of forms, from a task lasting a few hours to one taking weeks or even months. It is normal to provide the learner with the sources of information (i.e. links) so that the quest is not about searching the web but about comparing, contrasting, integrating and analysing information. Usually, the author of the quest provides assistance on how to proceed with the investigation. In some cases, the learner is asked to take on a particular role or the quest is designed as a group activity. The use of WebQuests is growing rapidly and they are being used at all levels of education.

▶ Learning materials

In e-Learning courses and programmes a key role is often played by the learning materials which can take a wide variety of forms and serve a

---

Activity   WebQuest

Using a search engine of your choice, carry out a search on the term 'WebQuest'. You will locate a variety of sites. Some will provide you with examples of different WebQuests. Compare and contrast the different examples you have located and produce a list of the different topics used for the quests for both adults and children.

Discussion

My search using the keyword WebQuest on the Google search engine gave 157 000 hits, which I reduced to 17 100 by searching within the original hits with the keyword 'example'. I considered the pages within the top 30 webpage hits. This produced a large number of examples for school children and students including: Natural history, Geography, Weather, Sport, Industry, Environment, Politics, Astronomy, Space travel, Modern and Ancient History, Music, Biology, Animals, Archaeology, Art, Mathematics, Finance, Reading, etc.

WebQuests clearly can be employed in almost every possible subject.

Table 4.3   Learning materials

Learning materials	How to use them	Comments
Study guide	A study guide will provide you with guidance from the course design team about how to obtain the most from the course. It will often explain the suggested route through the course materials, details of assessment and good practice.	It is useful to read the guide at the start of the course and to regularly review your progress against it. It can help you plan your learning.
Course website	Course websites often will provide information about: 1. outcomes of the course 2. course timetable 3. assessment methods 4. suggested materials 5. suggested links to other websites Changes to the course are often posted to the course site.	It useful to regularly visit the site to check for messages and new developments.
World wide web	Almost every topic is available on the world wide web. It should become a natural reaction to any question to search the web for information.	Search skills are a key requirement of any e-learner. Take every opportunity to practise. Although information on almost all subjects is available, its quality needs to be carefully assessed. Some e-learning courses will have identified many suitable world wide web resources to save you time and to assure you of their suitability.
Interactive learning materials (computer-based materials)	These materials are specifically created to help you learn. They are designed to assist you to realise specific learning outcomes and often clearly state what you should achieve by using them.	It is useful to take a few moments to ensure you understand the structure of the interactive materials. Many packages have an introduction to help you employ them effectively.

➜

Table 4.3   Learning materials – *continued*

Learning materials	How to use them	Comments
	Well-designed materials will engage you and assist you in assessing your own progress through tasks and questions.	
Open learning packs (paper-based materials)	These materials are specifically created to help you learn. They are designed to help you to complete specific learning outcomes and often clearly state what you should achieve by using them. Most open learning packs are paper-based materials that can be carried with you and studied when you have time.	It is useful to take a few moments to ensure you understand the structure of the materials. Large packs will often have several booklets, video/audio tapes and other materials. A few moments spent studying them is a useful investment to avoid later confusion. Many packages have an introduction or study guide to help you employ them effectively.
Text books	Text books are designed to provide an explanation of the whole or a part of the syllabus you are studying.	You can use a text book in a variety of ways, such as a reference into which you dip when you are unsure.
Learning resources	Learning resources can take many different forms including: 1. Lecture notes 2. Reading lists 3. Lists of websites 4. PowerPoint presentations 5. Videos 6. Examples of projects	The diverse nature of resources makes it difficult to generalise about using them. However, a key factor is to identify those parts that are most useful to you so that you can use those elements in revision or as content for essays/assignments. The use of learning resources is often called resource-based learning. It requires that the resources are effectively integrated to help you achieve the desired objectives. They also need to be supported with tutorials, peer discussions and feedback.
Problem-based learning	Problem-based learning is based on the concept that if you learn by doing then you	A powerful way of learning and especially useful in an organisational context where

➜

Table 4.3   Learning materials – *continued*

Learning materials	How to use them	Comments
	will retain the experience more effectively. The approach is based on asking you to solve a problem which is either provided for you or one which you identify for yourself. You will often be working with other students. The learning resources are provided and can take any form.	you are attempting to solve a business problem.
Case studies	These comprise a series of case studies of actual events that you are asked to study. They can be associated with any subject, but are often linked to business management.	The aim is to provide you with more experience by giving you access to case studies of events outside of your current practice. To gain the most benefit requires the case studies to be very detailed and for you to study them systematically, seeking common factors and to identify good practice to transfer to new situations.
Video lectures	These are short lectures filmed using a screen cam, edited from a longer video of a lecture or produced in other ways.	Short videos allow the tutor to provide brief inputs on difficult topics. They are useful in that they can be saved so you can view them several times and use them for revision.
Screen captures	There are several applications that allow the use of an application to be captured as a form of screen video.	These are essentially demonstrations of how to carry out a particular task using a software application. You should use them in a similar way. They have the advantage of being able to be viewed many times.

number of purposes. Table 4.3 describes a range of learning materials and how to use them.

▶ Blended learning

Many colleges, company training departments and other educational institutions are integrating e-learning approaches with more traditional methods. This can take a variety of forms such as:

- conventional lecture with teaching notes and visual aids placed on a college intranet for you to access;
- using digital cameras to record practical work for your portfolio of evidence;
- all assignments submitted in an electronic format and feedback provided in the form of annotation;
- email and conferencing with tutors in place of face-to-face tutorials;
- simulations of laboratory experiments as part of a conventional science course;
- distance learning course with regular face-to-face meetings.

There are a huge number of possibilities, and it is useful before you start any course to enquire about the methods that will be employed. The growth in blended learning is very rapid and probably exceeds pure e-learning approaches.

▶ Summary

1. **Places to learn**
    You can take part in e-learning in a number of locations including:

    - learning centres – colleges, training facilities and community sites have centres providing access to computers, communication technology and learning resources;
    - cybercafes – these take a variety of forms (e.g. internet kiosks and coffee bars);
    - mobile – laptop and notebook computers and PDAs combined with a mobile phone allow you to connect to the internet almost anywhere;

- home – create a suitable learning environment that is organised with your books, papers and other learning tools;
- workplace – at your desk or within the company's learning centre.

2. **Synchronous learning (e.g. audio or video conferencing)**
   Video and audio conferencing are synchronous approaches to e-learning. The technology varies from high quality large screen images, usually viewed by a group of learners, to individual learners interacting through to a small low quality image on a personal computer.

   Conferencing can take several forms such as:

- a group of students interacting together with a remote tutor;
- several groups of students in different locations interacting with a remote tutor;
- individual students at many different locations interacting with a remote tutor;
- large groups of students listening to a remote expert.

To obtain the best results, it is important that conferencing is organised and chaired. Special arrangements are sometimes required to allow learners to ask questions.

Synchronous conferencing learning is broadly similar to traditional classroom approaches.

3. **Groupware**
   Groupware is a form of synchronous interacting using an application that several participants can share. They can each take it in turn to control of the application. This is often used to undertake a group project.

4. **Managed Learning Environment (MLE) or Course Management System (CMS)**
   This is an online integration of a variety of systems to form an online environment. MLEs vary considerably but may offer:

- an administration system including financial, attendance and registration records;
- course information including learning resources, assessment systems, library, support and advice;

- communication systems such as email, conferencing, chat-rooms and bulletin boards.

5. Virtual Learning Environment (VLE) or Learning Management System (LMS)

A VLE essentially has the elements of an MLE that is intended to support and deliver online learning. VLEs are sometimes integrated into MLEs, but sometimes stand alone. There is no standard definition of an MLE or VLE.

6. World wide web

The world wide web is essentially a huge information library. It provides resources such as:

- libraries and book shops – catalogues and books online, including second-hand and out-of-print publications;
- electronic journals – there are many different journals, some are electronic copies of paper-based journals while others are only published online;
- online databases offer:
  - full-text – copies of the actual publication are available,
  - bibliographic – summary/abstracts of publications.

The world wide web provides many document files for you to download along with ebooks and other electronic documents. You should only download information if you have up-to-date virus protection. Some epublications require specific reader applications.

7. Intranets/extranets

Many colleges and companies have intranets which are essentially websites on the organisation's own network. These provide learners with access to facilities and information. An extranet is designed to be an intranet open to outside users through the use of a password and an agreed user identification.

8. WebQuest

WebQuests involve using the information available on the world wide web to achieve a set objective. The learner is often provided with the sources of information so they can concentrate on comparing, contrasting, integrating and analysing the information.

9. Learning materials

Learning materials are an important part of e-learning. A wide variety of materials are used including traditional forms, online information and interactive multimedia.

10. Blended learning

Blended learning is the integration of e-learning approaches with more traditional methods (e.g. simulations of laboratory experiments as part of a conventional science course).

5 e-Learning Skills

To be a successful, e-learners require well-developed learning skills. This chapter aims to help you realise the skills required of an e-learner. It will look at learning styles and strategies and how they relate to e-learning. A key factor in developing any skill is an awareness of your own performance of that skill. You need to recognise what you are doing and how well you are doing it. This will help you to improve your performance. All skills need practice in order to be developed and extended.

Initial experience

It is likely that you will go through a number of stages in your experience of e-learning. Initially, you are likely to feel unsure about what to do and how to use the resources available to you. This is not likely to last very long especially if you have a tutor, since he or she will be working to help you gain confidence and to understand the e-learning environment. A key factor is to start to communicate with other learners and your tutor using email, chatrooms or other methods. The more you can communicate, the quicker you will feel comfortable and confident. You need to gain an understanding of your subject, the environment, your tutor and the other learners. The best way of developing this is to ask questions, explore the subject content, reflect on the learning material and consider the answers.

Once you feel comfortable try to:

- develop your relationship with other learners and your tutor through communication technology;
- explore the learning environment – what is available (e.g. information about the assessment, learning content, etc.);
- collaborate with other learners;
- locate resources on the world wide web.

▶ Time management

One of the major benefits of e-learning is the freedom it gives you to learn at a time that fits into your life. However, the price of this freedom is that you must choose when to learn. In conventional courses you are given a timetable of classes that you must attend and assignments that you need to complete. This largely determines when you study. An e-learning course is likely to tell you, for example, that an estimated 150 hours of studying are required over a 22-week period (i.e. approximately 7 hours a week) with three assignments that provide 50% of the total marks required for the course, but the details of when you learn is left up to you. You can study as many hours a week as you like. You could do seven hours one day each week, one hour every day or any other combination that suits you. Some e-learning courses do not set a fixed period for completion, although these sorts of courses often do not lead to a qualification; with an open-ended course you only need to complete the content. The greatest risk of this type of programme is that you fall behind or fail to finish.

The timetable for a conventional course provides a structure which is supportive but limiting. E-learning increases the freedom but reduces the supportive structure. You must make the most of the freedom and replace the missing structure with your own. In order to do this you should:

- Consider the course structure – what do you need to do to complete the course (e.g. assignments, marks, examinations or other assessments).
- Analyse your own objectives and personal timetable (e.g. when do you want to finish the course?).
- Balance your different priorities against each other (e.g. childcare compared to study time; hours of employment – long work days make studying at weekends the only option and might mean limited access to computer technology).
- Reflect on your personal learning preferences – you may prefer to study at night or early in the morning.
- Recognise good-learning practice – it is poor practice to study for many hours without a break. It is better to study regularly, even if each session is relatively short, than to occasionally study for a long period.

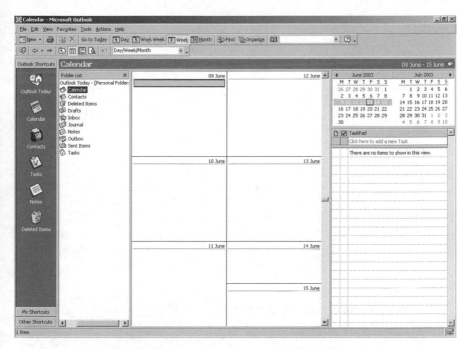

Figure 5.1 Microsoft Outlook

- Ensure your health and safety (e.g. eating and drinking at the computer is poor practice not least because you do not get a break, but also because liquids and electrical equipment do not mix).
- Consider family responsibilities – you must integrate your studies into the needs of your family (e.g. childcare).

Microsoft Outlook provides a number of features that allow you to organise and control your time. Figure 5.1 shows you the Calendar view within Outlook, which enables you to maintain an electronic diary of your studies. You can change your view of the calendar to show a single day, five-day week, seven-day week or a month by selecting the View menu (Figure 5.2). In addition to a calendar, Outlook provides a task pad to create a 'to do' list. These two functions offer a way of arranging your learning in a systematic way. Many organisations' Managed Learning Environments also provide calendars that course tutors will add key dates to, so it is useful to explore what your institution offers.

Figure 5.2 View menu

Activity   Create a study timetable

For your own course, devise a study timetable of significant aspects such as a major assignment or your regular study pattern. Consider all the issues, for example employment, preferences, social responsibilities, etc. Timetables are very helpful if they reflect your whole life and not simply the course.

Discussion

Figure 5.3 shows a simple example of a timetable developed using Microsoft Outlook. It is based on completing an assignment to write an essay about General Grant's career and involves allowing:

1. two periods to research the background for the essay;
2. two periods to write notes;
3. one period to prepare the essay;
4. one period to write the initial draft;
5. one period to revise and finalise the essay.

I have also allowed three days for unforeseen difficulties before the assignment has to be submitted.

   Within the timetable, I have also added when I will check my email. This shows a regular pattern of every other day. It is good practice to maintain contact with your peers and tutors, even when you are busy with an assignment. Personally, I check my email every day and sometimes more than once when I am busy. Many people assume you will respond to email messages immediately.

   To make it more useful, you should add your employment, family and other responsibilities since these will tell you if your study plan is realistic.

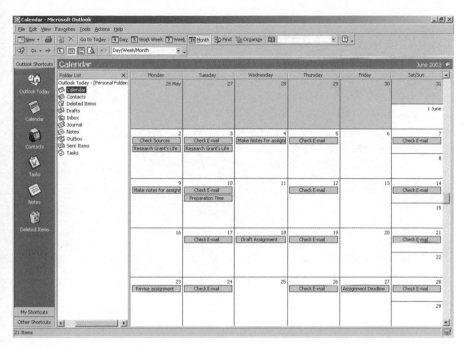

Figure 5.3   Timetable

► Acceptance of responsibility

All courses assume that you will accept responsibility for your actions, but will often provide structures to ensure that you cannot fall short simply because you forgot a deadline or something similar. In addition, e-learning courses also provide structural devices to help you. However, since you are often studying at a distance from your peers and tutors many of the informal systems, such as colleagues reminding you, are different. Tutors will frequently offer help or reminders at the end of lectures or workshops, but this is not so easily duplicated at a distance. e-Learning courses also offer more freedom and choice, so you are able to decide when you undertake particular tasks. This all combines to move responsibility onto you. Freedom comes with a price. You must understand:

- course structure and standards (e.g. alternatives);
- course conditions (e.g. who can grant an extension to a deadline and under what circumstances);

Activity   Review the structure of the course

Identify key dates and priorities – how are you going to ensure that you are able to fully satisfy the needs of the course? Write down an approach that will help you meet all the objectives.

Discussion

There are several different approaches that you might want to follow. One is to develop the 'Things to do' method which involves writing a list of things to do in relation to each key item in the course structure. Review the list regularly and cross off each step. Figure 5.4 illustrates the use of Microsoft Outlook to produce a list of tasks that need to be done in relation to preparing to write an essay about General Grant.

You may simply mark up a calendar or diary with key dates and tasks to act as your reminder. Microsoft Outlook, however, provides the means to give yourself electronic reminders.

How does your approach differ from these suggestions?

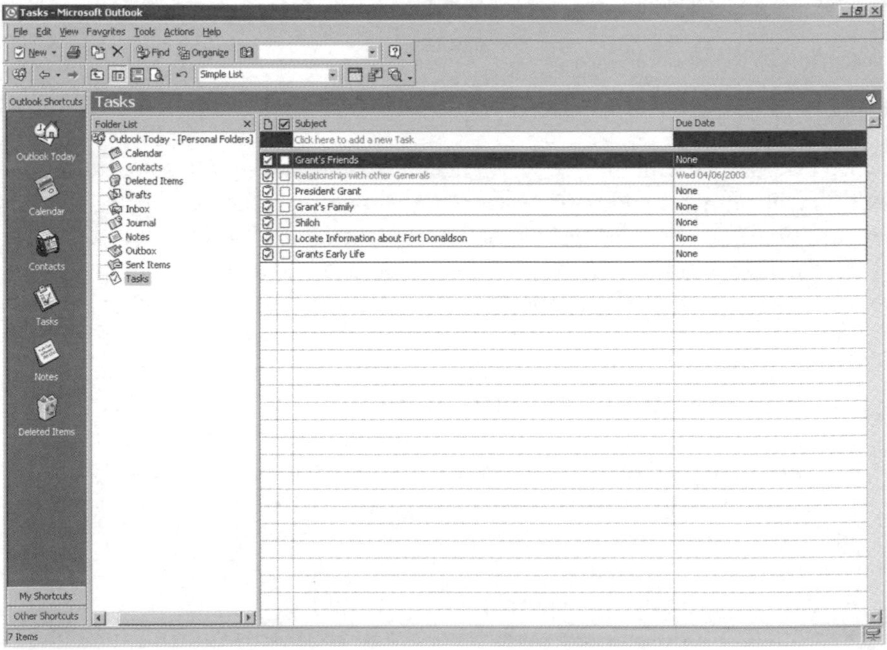

Figure 5.4   Tasks

- assessment conditions (e.g. pass marks, assessment methods – balance of continuous assessment and examinations);
- deadlines.

It is important when you are selecting at the start of the course to make yourself aware of these issues.

Acceptance of responsibility also includes realising your own personal objectives and standards. This can be expressed in a number of different ways, such as aiming to reach a standard that will equip you for a particular career.

▶ Planning

You have almost certainly met students who always seem to finish an assignment at the last moment. You may behave in this way yourself. It is poor practice. Almost certainly your performance will be reduced if you do not plan ahead. Planning will improve your results, you will be more productive and you will reduce your stress.

Planning involves:

- looking ahead:
  - what does the course require you to do over the next term?
  - what subjects will you be studying?
  - what assessments will you need to undertake?
- identifying critical points (e.g. two assessments close together – how can you prepare for both?);
- setting your goals – what do you want to achieve?
- producing your personal action plan:
  - when you will study?
  - starting your reading early enough
  - starting your preparation for an essay
- organising yourself:
  - creating records/files of your work,
  - balancing your life – good life/study balance;
- monitoring your performance;
- adjusting your plans.

Activity   Planning an assignment

Consider an assignment you need to complete:

1. When does it need to be submitted (i.e. the date)?
2. Working backwards, consider how long you will need to complete the assign-
    ment:
    – do you have all the information you will need or do you have to locate it
    – what research will you need to undertake?
    – how long will it take to write?
    – are there any compulsory elements (e.g. it is a group activity and you need to
      agree with the other members what each of you will do)?
3. What is your writing process?
    – outline notes,
    – initial draft,
    – proof read/spell and grammar check,
    – final draft.

If you have a real assignment, plan your timetable considering the issues above. If
you don't, then plan an essay of 3000 words about the main trends in the information society (e.g. employment changes, new skills, social changes, entertainment,
etc.). It is due in four weeks' time.

Discussion

Planning an essay on the main trends in the information society that needs to be
submitted in four weeks' time.

➔

► Self-assessment

There are lots of ways of judging your own progress. Some are formal
(e.g. marks achieved), while others are informal (e.g. comparing your
own understanding with your peers). The informal methods are often
part of discussions before or after a lecture or other learning activities,
where you can compare your own reactions with those of your peers.
When you are studying at a distance from your colleagues or you rarely
meet them, many of these informal methods are not apparently available to you. However, email provides a means of communicating with
all your peers in a far more systematic and potentially effective way
than a brief chat at the end of a presentation. It does, however, require
the confidence to ask the questions.

 In traditional learning courses, a key responsibility of the tutor is to
ensure that you are aware of your progress. Tutors will often speak to

Activity   Planning an assignment – *continued*

1. I do not have all the information that I will need. I must search the world wide web, library catalogue, bibliographic database or e-journals and then read, analyse and make notes about what I find. I estimate that will take a whole day and perhaps longer if I find a lot of information. I will need to split the task, since a whole day reading and researching is probably too much at one time.
2. With a good set of notes, I think I could write a 3000-word initial draft in two or three sessions of three hours. I doubt I could do more than one session on any day.
3. Proof reading and checking will take about three hours, but again I will need to break it up since I cannot redraft in a single session.
4. Final draft will take about three hours.

This tells me I need to divide the work on the assignment into about eight sessions. I have four weeks over which to plan the sessions. I will almost certainly have other tasks to do and a reasonable pattern is likely to be:

1. **Research and notes** – two sessions during week 1;
2. **Initial draft** – three sessions of three hours during week 2;
3. **Proof reading** – two sessions during week 3;
4. **Final draft** – one session during week 3 or 4 (allows you some time if things go wrong).

A task such as writing an essay, which can be difficult for many students, can benefit from planning. Many learners who do not plan will find themselves in week 4 trying to fit everything in and subjecting themselves to intense pressure and the possibility of submitting a poor assignment.

each learner individually to highlight good work, any weaknesses, misunderstandings and confusion. In e-learning this responsibility is moved to you. Tutors are still responsible for providing feedback, but this is likely to have changed from a verbal face-to-face process to written feedback. Face-to-face allows you to immediately ask straight-forward questions about your performance, whereas written feedback requires you to make the additional effort of contacting the tutor. However, it is important to be clear so ask for clarification if the feed-back leaves you uncertain.

It is useful to keep records of all forms of feedback, since this will make the judging progress easier. It will help you to identify subject areas that need more work and those where you are making progress and allow you to address problem areas.

A wide range of assessment approaches are used within e-learning materials (Clarke, 2001b; Race, 1994). They include:

- multiple choice questions;
- true or false questions;
- sorting information into order;
- matching pieces of information together;
- filling in the gaps.

These methods are also used in more conventional paper-based learning materials. However, there are some methods that are uniquely used in online or e-learning assessment such as:

- taking part in a virtual journey or exploring an environment;
- using a simulation;
- developing an electronic portfolio.

Many assessments are intended to help you check your own understanding rather than making up part of the formal assessment process and you will often be given the opportunity to take such assessments

Activity   Self-assessment

Assessing your own progress is an essential element in all forms of learning but especially in online courses, where you are studying independently and at a distance from your peers and tutors.

Consider your own experience of all forms of learning and develop a list of how you assess your own progress.

Discussion

There are a variety of ways of assessing progress, but some you may have mentioned are:

1. results from assignments, exercises and other activities;
2. comparing your own performance with other students (both formally in examinations and in informal situations such as in discussion);
3. feedback from tutors – this can take various forms but includes:

   – marks and comments on assignments, essays, etc.,
   – individual tutorials,
   – comments to other learners in seminars;

4. listening to questions and answers in a tutorial.

Some of these activities have an online equivalent, some do not.

more than once. To take advantage of this type of assessment, it is useful to keep records of patterns that show your strengths and weaknesses.

Portfolios

A widely-used assessment method is the portfolio, that is, a collection of evidence to demonstrate your skills, understanding and competency in a particular subject. The evidence is defined by the awarding body or the educational institution, so that each learner's portfolio can be compared and measured against a standard. It is often aligned with the detailed requirements of the course or qualification being undertaken. Typical evidence requirements are:

* examples of work undertaken (e.g. letters you have sent to show you can lay out and present an effective communication, minutes taken by you and copies of papers you have written, orders placed

---

Activity e-Portfolios

Using a search engine of your own choice locate a variety of sites covering the use and development of e-portfolios and consider how they are being employed.

Discussion

My initial approach to this search was to use the simple term 'e-portfolio', then I added the word 'learning' (i.e. e-portfolio learning). I found a large number of webpages showing e-portfolios being used internationally and in a variety of ways. Several sites offered you the opportunity to see examples of student portfolios.
  Different ideas for e-portfolios covered:

1. Showing personal, continuous, professional development in a dynamic way as we are all lifelong learners.
2. Helping artists and performers to exhibit their skills and achievements through digital music, video and photographs.
3. Providing templates for particular courses, topics or subjects to assist learners to produce their portfolios.
4. Showing student progress since e-portfolios are dynamic and will change as the course continues.
5. Reducing the costs of conventional portfolios.
6. Providing standards for e-portfolios so that learners' work can be compared and assessed.

There were many other ideas and concepts being explored and developed, indicating the large degree of interest in this approach.

after a sales demonstration, photographs of work completed (e.g. window displays, products constructed etc.);

- supervisor's, tutor's or mentor's witness statements (e.g. colleague describing how you undertook a particular task);
- observations undertaken by objective observers (e.g. assessment of your performance in carrying out an experiment).

ICT provides the opportunity to develop electronic portfolios that can take a variety of forms. A simple collection of evidence would include:

- copies of word-processed documents (e.g. creative writers);
- digital photographs (e.g. artists, craftsmen and gardeners);
- emails (e.g. to show your participation in group tasks);
- audio and video evidence of your competence (e.g. musicians).

In some cases, an e-portfolios could be a personal website designed to show the person's skills, knowledge, competencies and achievements. This type of portfolio is essentially a living document of the candidate's achievements. The portfolio can be updated and enhanced from anywhere. It becomes a dynamic document.

Virtual experiments
The potential to create virtual environments for learners to explore, carry out experiments and undertake tasks is being exploited in e-learning courses. The practical issues of health and safety for students with no experience of a laboratory, the cost of operating laboratories

---

Activity   Virtual experiments

Using a search engine of your own choice, locate a variety of sites covering the use and development of virtual experiments and consider how they are being employed. Example:

- Physical Science Information Gateway offers access to many internet resources. Explore what is offered – www.psigate.ac.uk/

Discussion

A simple search of the phrase 'Virtual Experiments' identified many sites that offered information about them and also many examples of experiments. If you extend the search using a subject name (e.g. virtual experiments physics) you will find experiments in various different scientific subjects, such as chemistry, physics, engineering, mathematics and astronomy.

Activity   Undertake a virtual experiment

Identify a virtual experiment that you can use and then undertake it. Reflect on the experience.

Examples:
- Try the genetics experiments available on the Channel Four Television website www.channel4.com/learning/microsites/G/genetics/activities/buglab.html. This experiment requires Macromedia Shockwave Player which is available free through the site.
- Try the robots animations and experiments available from the BBC Television website www.bbc.co.uk/learning/courses/
- Virtual micrometer – learn how to use a micrometer http://members.shaw.ca/ron.blond/Micrometer.APPLET/

Discussion

Your experience will depend on the experiment you have chosen, but you may have found that you are able to explore more different options than you probably could have done in the real world. It may have allowed you to recover from errors which, in an actual experiment, would have cost you time and forced you to start again.

What did you experience? How does it compare with your previous experience of undertaking actual experiments? Did you learn a lot about the subject?

If you have time, try carrying out several different experiments.

and the potential for practical work to go wrong have all encouraged the development of virtual experiments.

Virtual experiments enable you to experience more than if you carried them out in a real laboratory, since you can revise the experience to explore all the possibilities and do so without leaving your home or learning centre.

Formal assessment

All the self-assessment methods that we have been considering can be used for more formal assessment by your college, employer or the qualification awarding body. Some other ways of assessing your performance you may encounter are:

- video and audio conferencing;
- remote control or monitoring.

The examiner and student can be separated in space but linked through video or audio conferencing, which can be used to provide a form of oral or demonstration assessment. The student is asked to make a presentation, complete a task or take part in a role play. The examiner can watch or listen to the student and then ask questions.

Remote control or monitoring is often part of technical courses and allows the examiner to view the students' computer display while they are carrying out a task. This allows them to assess progress directly, offer feedback or take control of the computer and demonstrate how to carry out the task.

Evaluation

Another aspect of assessment is consideration of the effectiveness of the e-learning course. This will almost certainly involve you, if only to ask you what you liked or disliked about the programme.

If your college or employer is seeking to evaluate the e-learning course you may, for example, be asked to complete a questionnaire at the end of the course enquiring about your views of the course, assess what you have learnt or take part in evaluation interviews. e-Learning is a relatively new approach, so it is perhaps more likely to be evaluated than other more conventional approaches.

▶ Problem solving

All forms of learning require students to deal with the many practical problems that emerge. e-Learning students are often working in isolation, dependent on information and communication technology.

Technical problems

Technology can be confusing and frustrating when it does not work. This does not mean that you need to become a computer technician to be a successful e-learner. You need to know where to find help to solve the problem. This section aims to help you access assistance, particularly if you are studying at a distance from your college or at home. However, if you only use your college or employer's equipment, it is likely that you need only report that the machine is not working correctly.

If technology goes wrong at home, you can feel isolated and vulnerable. Good technical support is vital to e-learning and many educational providers offer telephone and other forms of helpline. At an early stage in your course you need to find out precisely what help is on offer and how you access it. In some cases, technical assistance will only be available between certain hours and on specific days (e.g. 9 a.m. to 5 p.m. Monday to Friday).

In many cases, the help system is a telephone line with a technical specialist who can diagnose the problem and suggest solutions. You need to be willing and able to undertake the solution. This will often mean, in the case of hardware faults, sending the computer back to the supplier (it is good practice to keep the original packaging). With software faults it will probably require re-installing applications. The specialist will talk you through the process, but you need to be able to carry out their advice.

Help desks will usually only provide support for products they have supplied. A college helpdesk will provide advice on the Managed Learning Environment and associated products, but will not help you with your own computer. You will need to contact the supplier's help desk for assistance with your own equipment.

Online communication problems can be difficult to diagnose and often involve trying out different solutions. This is difficult if you have only a single telephone line because you cannot talk to the helpline and connect to the internet at the same time? It will help if you have two lines or a mobile phone so that you can discuss the problem while trying out solutions. Many internet service providers offer technical support as an alternative to your educational provider. The scope of the technical help will depend on your contract and can involve additional costs, so you need to check your contract. In some cases it will be 24 hours a day everyday of the year.

Some help lines also offer a website containing solutions to standard problems or informing you of problems outside your control (e.g. that college computer servers have broken down). It is useful to check online sources before telephoning the technical support team. To take advantage of all forms of technical support you need to be prepared. Some useful things to remember are:

- have all your documentation accessible:
  - user identification (help lines will only help if you can show you are a registered student or customer),
  - computer handbooks/users manuals/warranty/guarantees (e.g. computer, monitor, modem and printers)
- write down a precise description of what is going wrong, including any error messages that have appeared;
- keep a notebook with a record of what you have tried;
- label the many cables and connections on your computer system to avoid becoming confused;

Activity   Microsoft Windows

Microsoft Windows operating system provides help and support to users enabling you to become familiar with the system. You will benefit from technical assistance if you understand the fundamentals about your operating system. All versions of Microsoft Windows offer a help system, some provide a troubleshooting option and some a guided tour to the system.

Explore the help system provided by your operating system.

Discussion

I explored the Help and Support system provided by Microsoft XP Home Edition. Figure 5.5 shows the Help window containing an option to help you fix a problem. Figure 5.6 shows the display if you select the Fix a Problem option. A list of problem types lets you choose a category. The process systematically asks you to identify precisely what is wrong. This is done by offering you lists of options (questions) for you to select and then focus on the problem itself. Eventually you will be offered advice to help you solve the problem. You can print this advice and it is useful to keep a copy either for future reference or to explain to the technical help line.

Other options in the Help and Support system will offer you a tour or tutorial of the operating system (Figure 5.7). This is a good way to gain familiarity with your operating system.

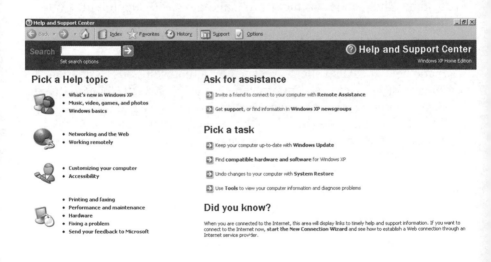

Figure 5.5   Windows XP Help System

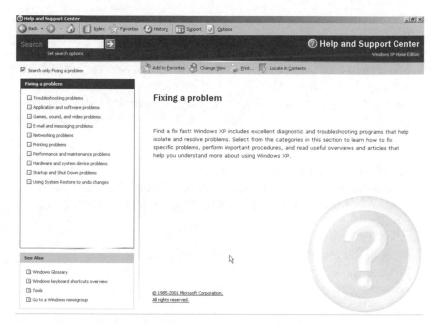

Figure 5.6   Fixing a problem

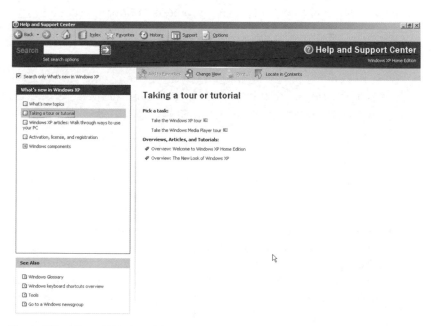

Figure 5.7   Tour of Windows XP

- become familiar with the operating system and diagnostic information so you can follow the technical help line's advice;
- keep all your installation disks, those containing equipment drivers and other software near to your computer in an ordered way so you can rapidly locate them;
- although it may seem obvious, it is always worth checking that your power connections are correct and that all other connections are firm.

Other forms of problems

Using technology involves getting used to solving problems, but many aspects of learning also involve unravelling dilemmas. You need to be able to:

- identify the real problem (i.e. not the symptoms);
- analyse the evidence systematically;
- consider if there is a pattern or an exception to the rule;
- review the solution;
- apply your experience (i.e. learning from similar problems you have already encountered).

There are a variety of ways of solving problems. Some approaches are:

- **Trial and error** – although this method appears to rely on good luck to provide the solution, if you systematically make changes and notice the effects of each change then it can be useful. However, it does depend on making changes logically and noting the effects, otherwise it becomes guesswork. This method can also take a lot of time.
- **Serendipity** – essentially you are hoping that some inspiration will occur to provide a solution.
- **Analytical** – this is the approach adopted in the activity (i.e. gathering the facts, analysing the evidence, balancing the information to arrive at a solution and finally reviewing the solution).
- **Creative** – there are a variety of techniques that can be employed to solve problems creatively, such as brainstorming.
- **Rule book** – this is a standard approach where set procedures are followed (e.g. soldiers are often encouraged to follow the rule book, which is basically the experience of many earlier soldiers written down for the benefit of others).

Activity   How do you solve problems?

Consider how you approached some recent problems. They can be anything, such as your car failing to start, poor results for a piece of work you were sure was well done or a misunderstanding with someone. Think through a range of problems and write down how you handled them.

Discussion

A standard approach to problem solving can be summarised as:

1. Identify the problem (e.g. flat battery, wet engine or poor connection).
2. Get the facts – find out as much information as you can about the problem.
3. Analyse the evidence.
4. Decide on a solution (e.g. charge battery, telephone breakdown service or fix the connection).
5. Check the solution.

What is your approach?

▶ Coping with stress

Everyone finds learning stressful at times – perhaps you are facing an examination, have left it too late to finish an assignment or simply find the subject difficult to understand. e-Learning provides more freedom to study when you want, at the pace that suits you and at your preferred location. This can also mean trying to learn in the family home with many distractions around you, combining your studies with family responsibilities and studying for long hours when perhaps you should be relaxing or even sleeping. It is vital for your health to establish a good life and study balance. If you are also working, the balance becomes even more complex because you have to consider work, life and learning.

A key factor in coping with stress is to try to identify the cause and to remove it. If you have family responsibilities combined with a heavy learning burden, you will almost certainly feel stressed from time to time. If you find yourself with a deadline to meet and have to work more many hours (perhaps all night) to get the work done, then you are going to experience substantial pressure.

Some ways to cope with stress are:

- Before you start your course find out what is expected of you. Consider your own personal circumstances and judge whether you can deal with that amount of commitment. Many courses will provide you with guidance about how much time you should expect to study each week.
- Planning your work will reduce stress by avoiding some of the

Activity   Life, work and study balance

Over a typical week, keep a detailed record of how you spend your time. This should include:

1. All activities you spend time on – with your family, eating, relaxing, sleeping, studying and working
2. When you undertake each activity (e.g. 1 a.m. to 2 a.m. – writing essay)
3. Present your analysis as a calendar with a time table

Example:

Date: 29 June Sunday
8 a.m.   Breakfast
8.30 a.m.   Walk to local shop
8.45 a.m.   Read newspaper

Analyse the record to identify how much time you spend:

1. studying;
2. working;
3. relaxing/social life;
4. sleeping.

What is the balance?

Discussion

It is difficult to say what makes a good balance of work, life and study. Everyone has a different mix of family responsibilities, work pressures and learning activities to combine, but you should be able to see a distinct pattern. The key is that everything should be in moderation and extremes should be unusual. Some features to be concerned about are:

1. you have very little social life;
2. all your studying takes place late at night;
3. you do not see your family on many days (e.g. Monday to Friday);
4. you get less than eight hours sleep a night;
5. you get little or no exercise;
6. you are not studying regularly.

crises that generate pressure, for example giving yourself sufficient time to complete assignments without last-minute panics.

- e-Learning provides you with more freedom to study, but does expect you to take more responsibility for your learning. Use the freedom to plan your studies and reduce the pressure.
- Give yourself a sound study pattern with regular breaks, rests and meal breaks. It may sound great to study all night, but it is both poor learning practice and unhealthy. It is better to study for shorter periods but regularly. An hour a day is likely to be more effective than seven hours once a week.
- Different learning tasks need different study patterns, so be flexible. It is unreasonable to expect to read books for a whole day and then get concerned because you are unproductive. You are likely to get better results if you try to work on a range of different tasks.
- Monitor your life and study balance to ensure that you are not neglecting your learning in favour of a busy social life or, equally, ignoring relaxation in favour of studying.
- Online learning can be very isolating and this can add stress to your learning. At an early stage of the course, try to make contact with other learners so that you develop relationships and give yourself some peer support. Problems can often be reduced by some friendly discussion.
- Ask for help when you have a problem. Many tutors comment that they can be more helpful to their students if they are informed earlier of difficulties, but frequently they are asked for assistance too late.
- Assessment makes most learners anxious. The key is to prepare yourself adequately for the test by planning ahead and to give yourself enough time to revise or complete the assessed task.

▶ Motivation

There are many reasons for undertaking an e-learning course. You might want:

- to get a better job;
- to give yourself more job security;
- to change your life;
- to learn about a subject that fascinates you.

Whatever the reasons for learning, almost all students find there are

Activity Motivation

Consider the course of study you are currently undertaking and write a list of the reasons for studying it.

Next, consider the times when your motivation is low – what demotivates you and what helps you to overcome these periods.

Discussion

At one stage in my life I undertook nine years' part-time study while completing masters and doctorate courses. My reasons for this long period of effort were:

1. a real interest in the subjects I was studying;
2. developing expertise in areas relevant to my career;
3. developing my own self-esteem;
4. discovering my own strengths.

The factors that demotivated me always seemed to be centred around poor or slow progress. In my case, success made me want to achieve more while a delay or an obstacle often discouraged me. I overcame these periods by taking a break from the frustration to reflect on what had gone wrong. I was often able to see a new way of overcoming the barrier.

times when they are miserable, irritated with their own performance or the technology (especially true of e-learning) or simply unsure if they are doing the right course. A motivated learner will overcome problems and difficulties, while a demotivated person will be hindered by even the smallest of barriers.

When motivation is low, it is important to take action to improve your enthusiasm. Try some of the following steps:

- have a break – a few hours away from studying can often work wonders, while trying to force yourself to study when motivation is low will often achieve little;
- remember why you are doing this course – there is nothing like recalling your original motivation to disperse the doubts;
- consider what you have already achieved, what you will gain by completing the course and how little there is still to do;
- email your tutor and ask for help;
- email other learners and see how they feel – they are in the best position to understand what you are experiencing;
- discuss how you feel with your family – often their support is vital to successful learning.

▶ Reflection

Reflection is an important learning skill in all forms and types of learning. It will help you gain a new insight into yourself and the subjects you are studying. Everyone can reflect on experiences in an informal and haphazard way; to gain the maximum benefit, it is useful to approach it in a systematic and considered way.

Normally, reflection requires peace and relaxation, yet many people are able to reflect on a bus or train. You need some mental space to reflect and that is often available during a journey. Other ways of gaining the space are to:

- take a walk in the countryside – or in a town, although there are more potential distractions and interruptions in an urban area;
- listen to some favourite music – headphones are an effective way of cutting yourself off from the world;
- sit in the sun by yourself;
- find a quiet place (e.g. library);
- make notes about the subject and later review them.

When you reflect you are trying to:

- consider new experiences in the context of what you already know;

Activity   Reflect on reflection

Consider your own efforts to think through issues – that is, how you have found reflecting. What is the best way for you to concentrate on thinking through a set of ideas, comparing different experiences or trying to understand an issue? What environment do you need to reflect effectively? How do you have to approach the task?

Discussion

Personally, I am able to reflect in different settings depending on my personal motivation and the subject that I am considering. My best environment for reflecting on new knowledge is to take a walk with a notebook and focus on the different aspects as I stroll. As ideas or concepts occur to me, I stop and make a few notes so that I do not forget them.

You may find that you need a particular setting such as a quiet room or library in order to reflect. You may need to take notes and look at these a little later. Many people find that a short break after reflecting gives them new insights into the topic. It is useful to know your own reflection preferences so that you can get the maximum benefit from the experience.

- fit new knowledge into the existing understanding that you have about the subject;
- analyse your e-learning experience perhaps by comparing it with your previous experiences of learning in more traditional ways.

Reflection helps you to understand new information, to fit it into what you already know and to change your own opinions.

▶ Research skills

Research skills form a part of all courses. You may only wish to find out the answer to a question, find examples to help you write an essay or revise a topic for an examination, but they all involve locating and

---

Activity   Research skills

Consider searching for information about Online Assessment:

1. Plan your research – what would you like to find?
2. What search terms will you use and what engines?

Carry out the search and record the most successful results (e.g. webpages, etc.)

Discussion

My initial step was to check out the scale of the task by simply searching the world wide web using three different search engines – Google, Yahoo and MSN. The results indicated that there is a massive number of webpages linked to the subject:

- Google – 3 020 000 pages
- Yahoo – 2 790 000 pages
- MSN – 1 321 753 pages

To concentrate the search I amended the terms to E-learning Online Assessment and this reduced the number of pages significantly:

- Google – 140 000 pages
- Yahoo – 121 000 pages
- MSN – 33 508 pages

I next reviewed the top ten pages from all three engines and found that both Google and Yahoo had the same ones, while MSN had only a single page in common with the other two. I would have then explored the ten sites to help refine my search terms.
  What did you do and what were the outcomes?

evaluating information. Earlier you considered how to search for information on the world wide web, which is a key skill, but there are many
associated activities. The list in Table 5.1 outlines some good practices
to help your research activities.

One approach extensively employed when the world wide web was
relatively new was to email a famous or well-known researcher or
author with a question. This was very successful when they received
only an occasional message but nowadays all users of email receive
large volumes of messages. You are unlikely to receive any response
except an occasional acknowledgement. However, many researchers
and authors have developed personal websites including details of
their publications, ideas and new projects. These are very useful when
you are seeking information. In a similar way, many research groups
have created websites to disseminate the outcomes of their projects.

▶ Summary

1. **Initial experience**
   - Participate in all communication activities to develop your rela-
     tionship with other learners and your tutor.
   - Explore the learning environment – discover what is available to
     help – look for learning materials, study guides, library facilities
     and other resources.

2. **Time management**
   - A major benefit of e-learning is the freedom to learn when it is
     best for you, but this comes at the price of being responsible for
     managing your own time.
   - Microsoft Outlook and similar applications provide you with a
     means of managing your time efficiently.
   - Consider the course requirements and structure (e.g. assign-
     ments, marks, examinations or other assessments).
   - Analyse your own objectives, personal timetable and learning
     preferences.
   - Balance your priorities against each other (e.g. family and work
     responsibilities).
   - Consider good learning and health practice.
   - Devise your own study timetable and review it at intervals.

Table 5.1   Research activities

Practice	Explanation	Discussion
1. Question	The first step is to develop/ consider the question that your research is seeking to answer.	You may feel that the question is obvious but try to write a precise statement of it. Some time spent considering the actual question you want to address will save you time later.
2. Plan	Before you start to research your subject consider what you are seeking to find: • general information introducing the subject; • surveys – quantitative or qualitative; • research reports; • particular authors.	It is very tempting to go immediately online and to start searching. However, this is likely to be less effective than spending a few minutes simply considering what you are seeking.
3. Search terms	You need to consider a range of terms and alternatives that you might use. Consider the use of the Boolean terms to refine your search: • OR • AND • NOT Everyone has a favourite search engine but it is often beneficial to employ more than one to provide a comparison	There are two alternative approaches to searching: 1. Start broad and focus. It is often useful to start your search with general terms especially if it is a new subject or topic since this will capture the most sources. Subsequent searches can focus on the precise area of your interest. You might want to consider a series of searches, each one building on the previous one. 2. Start focused and broaden if you cannot locate sufficient sources ➜

Table 5.1 Research activities – *continued*

Practice	Explanation	Discussion
4. Assessing the quality of information	Who is the author? Is biographical information provided? Who owns the site (e.g. consider the domain). Are they appropriate for the information provided? Is it a personal site? Is it simply an individual's opinion? What references are incorporated within the information? What links are provided from the page? Are they good quality pages? When was the site last updated?	The earlier section on the quality of world wide web information should be consulted.
5. Review the results of the search	You need to review the outcome of your search, since this will indicate not only the success of your efforts but also suggest other keywords and sites to refine your search.	Reflection and review are important elements in any research process.
6. Saving results and searches	You will often need to repeat searches, so keep records of the outcomes and search terms.	Keeping records is a vital element in research. You will feel stupid if you are unable to find information later that was previously very helpful to you.

3. **Acceptance of responsibility**
    *   e-Learning assumes that you accept more responsibility for your studies than you would with traditional learning methods in that it gives you more freedom over how and when to learn.
    *   Understand the course structure, standards and conditions (e.g. deadlines and assessment) from the start.
    *   Microsoft Outlook and similar applications can be helpful with planning studies (e.g. to do lists).

4. **Planning**
    *   Planning will improve your results, productivity and reduce your stress.
    *   Planning involves:
        *   looking ahead,
        *   identifying critical points,
        *   setting goals,
        *   producing a personal action plan,
        *   organising yourself.
    *   Plan assignments and other components as well as the overall course.

5. **Self-assessment**
    You are responsible for monitoring your own progress.

    *   Compare your own progress/understanding with that of your colleagues – contact them early in the course and try to establish a culture of self-help.
    *   Question any feedback to ensure you have a clear understanding of your strengths and weaknesses.
    *   Interactive materials often offer many self-test methods which you should employ to help you assess your own understanding.
    *   Reflect on all forms of feedback you receive.
    *   Keep records of feedback/performance so you can identify patterns of strengths and weaknesses.
    *   e-Portfolios are a means of dynamically showing your skills, understanding and competency.
    *   Virtual experiments allow you to revise and experience a large range of experiments.

6. **Problem solving**
    It is a normal part of using technical equipment that occasionally

you will encounter problems with the hardware or software, so be aware that:

- Courses will provide assistance to solve problems and you need to know how you can access that help.
- Technical specialists will often talk you through the trouble-shooting process with both hardware and software problems.
- Online communication problems often require two telephone lines so the technical support can check your connection to the internet while you are still able to talk to them.
- Both your internet service and educational provider can provide technical support. The degree of support will depend on your contracts with them.
- Help line websites often present solutions to standard problems or provide background information.
- It is useful to have all your documents, handbooks, passwords and tools close to your computer.
- It is important to make notes of exactly what is not working, especially error messages.
- You should always disconnect the equipment from the power supply before opening the case or working inside the computer or other equipment.
- Operating systems often have extensive help systems.

7. **Coping with stress**
    Stress affects all learners at some time during their course. However, there are a variety of ways of helping yourself to cope with stress:

    - e-Learning provides you with more freedom to study but does expect you to take more responsibility for your learning. Use the freedom to plan your studies and reduce the pressure.
    - Establish a good life and study balance (i.e. rest, relaxation, work and family).
    - Remove the causes of stress.
    - Plan your studies and your life.
    - Build relationships with your fellow learners.
    - Ask your tutor for help if you need it.

8. Motivation

Motivation is critical for success in most courses. Everyone gets demotivated at some stage. The key is not to ignore the problem but to take action to overcome the feelings (e.g. take a break, consider what you have already achieved and reflect on why you are doing the course).

9. Reflection

If you are able to reflect effectively on your own experiences and understanding, you will gain a significant learning benefit. Reflection requires:

- a systematic and considered approach;
- mental space (e.g. peace and quiet).

10. Research skills

Research skills are useful in almost all learning programmes and are vital for the efficient and effective use of the world wide web as an information source. Research requires you to:

- plan your investigation;
- search for information, perhaps using the web (e.g. identify appropriate keywords);
- assess the quality of the information you find;
- review your approach: has it been effective? Should you try another way?
- save your keywords and outcomes since you may want to repeat the search.

6 Developing Skills

This chapter continues the development of skills discussed in Chapter 5, along with further chapters. It will focus on providing a range of activities to extend your e-learning skills.

▶ Time management

There is often a considerable difference between how you think you employ your time and how you actually do. It is important to be aware of this difference since it will help you plan and manage your time. The activity below asks you to monitor how you spent your time over a week-long period.

Activity   Monitor your use of time

Over a period of a week keep detailed records of how you spend your time. Figure 6.1 gives an example of a table which may help you keep your records, but feel free to modify it to suit your own pattern. It is simply a breakdown of a day spent study-ing showing learning, breaks and social activities. You may want to add comments on whether you felt the learning went well (e.g. you could concentrate on achieved good results), travel time or any other significant action that requires your time.

	Date	21-Jul-03			
	Start Time	Finish Time	Activity	Notes	Total
	8:00:00 AM	10:00:00 AM	Reading and making notes		2 hours
	10:00:00 AM	10:30:00 AM	Break		0.5 hours
	10:30:00 AM	13:00:00 PM	Research on the Internet	Sources for essay on Napolean	2.5 hours
	13:00:00 PM	14:30:00 PM	Break		1.5 hours
	14:30:00 PM	17:00:00 PM	Library	Visit to library to locate some books and journals	2.5 hours
	17:00:00 PM	20:00:00 PM	Break	Dinner - doing nothing	2.5 hours
	20:00:00 PM	22:00:00 PM	Television	Watching football match	2 hours
	22:00:00 PM	23:30:00 PM	Listening to music		1.5 hours
	23:30:00 PM		Bed		
Summary					
Study Time					6.5 hours
Breaks					4.5 hours
Social Activities					3.5 hours

Figure 6.1   Monitoring time   ➜

Activity   Monitor your use of time – *continued*

Discussion

Most people underestimate how much time they spend simply doing nothing or what could loosely be called social activities. Equally, it is essential to take regular breaks. Your productivity will be improved if you do this. It is not sensible to try and study for many hours continuously. Make a drink, take a walk or simply watch the television. A regular pattern of short spells of studying is often very productive.

Assess how you spend your time. If your course provides guidance on how many hours you should study, compare the actual with the theory. Are you spending your precious time sensibly? Are you giving enough time to the most important work? Are you meeting your deadlines? Are you getting enough sleep? Are you studying at the most effective time (i.e. when you are alert)?

Are you finding that studying at certain times (e.g. evening) is difficult? Perhaps you are easy to distract at that time. It is often a good idea if you are finding that a particular time is a poor time for studying to switch to another (e.g. from evenings to mornings after breakfast).

Activity   To Do lists

A very useful task to assist your control and management of your time is making a To Do List. Simply list everything you need to do and then place the items in order of importance. This gives you a sequence of actions to move forward with your studies and helps you to make effective use of your time.

Write a To Do List of what you need to achieve over the next few weeks or months.

Discussion

I have produced my own list below, with an explanation of why each entry is important.

1. Essay – the deadline is only two weeks away and it is worth 20% of the continuous assessment for the course.
2. Locate the set books for the course – I need some of them almost immediately but it may take time since some of the books might have to be ordered.
3. Check the assessment criteria for the final examination – although this is some time ahead I need to consider my planning.
4. Email all the other members of my co-operative learning group to check if anyone else is finding understanding the course's fourth activity difficulty – although the deadline for the activity is some weeks away people often do not reply immediately and I need to clarify what I have to do.
5. Buy some floppy disks – not very important but I keep forgetting to do it.

Sometimes my lists are far longer and I frequently list tasks in the wrong order, but normally I get everything done without last-minute panics.

▶ Acceptance of responsibility

On a traditional course the responsibility for your learning is to some extent shared by your tutors, in that they will often organise the learning around assessment deadlines, plan time for revision and generally direct your attention to what they regard as critical activities. This process, although helpful, often conditions you to react to their initiatives rather than encouraging you to be proactive and take the lead.

One way of developing a more personal responsibility for your own learning is to take the lead. The next two activities are based on your volunteering to take responsibility for your own and, to some extent, other peoples' learning.

Activity　Volunteer to lead a group task

Collaborating with other learners to carry out a task is a frequent e-learning activity. It involves dividing responsibility for the component parts of the task between the group and asking people to take responsibility for roles such as leading the group.

In the next group activity volunteer to lead. While you undertake the task, keep a record/diary of what happens and reflect on the process and your own learning.

Discussion

Your experience will be unique to the circumstances of your group and task but you may have experienced:

1. It was easy to volunteer. Everyone accepted you – often people are reluctant to take responsibility so are happy if someone else comes forward.
2. It was not so easy getting agreement to everyone taking a fair share of the work, but you were pleased that a timetable was agreed.
3. Some group members have failed to meet their targets. In some cases, members do not seem to have done anything, others have done a lot but not what was agreed and a few have completed their agreed tasks.
4. You are spending a lot of effort encouraging members to keep to the agreement. This is not always successful.
5. You are working harder than you imagined.
6. You find yourself filling some of the gaps.
7. Other group members help by taking on extra work.

Overall you have probably learnt a great deal about the problems of co-ordinating a group without any authority to compel. However, there is a lot of satisfaction in achieving the end result. You are also surprised as much by who helped as who did not pull their weight.

Hopefully you have learnt a good deal about yourself and how you should behave in a learning group.

Another typical e-learning activity is online or mailgroup discussions. Many people tend to show a reluctance to take part. A useful way of developing your own acceptance of responsibility is to play an active part in an online discussion.

Activity   Participate in an online discussion

Prepare yourself to take part in a discussion that you start and make a significant contribution to. Remember that a discussion is more that just giving your own views. It requires other learners to take part and you need to be prepared to help others to contribute. While you are involved in the discussion, keep a record/diary of what happens and reflect on the process and your own learning.

Discussion

Your own experience will be different from these reflections, since it will be a unique experience based on the topic and the membership of discussion group. However, you may have encountered:

1. A slow response to your original message.
2. Responses that seemed only marginally related to your contribution.
3. Responses that showed considerable understanding of the issues and made you feel inadequate and reluctant to reply for fear of showing your own lack of knowledge.
4. The need to email other learners directly to ask a specific question about their contribution.
5. The need to email other learners to encourage them to take part.
6. Messages that relate to much earlier contributions taking the discussion off at a tangent.
7. Messages sent directly to you asking for clarification or to encourage you to keep contributing.
8. Contributions that are unconnected to the topic.

Many other things may have happened. Hopefully you have gained confidence in your ability to contribute to discussions and have learnt about yourself.

► Planning

Planning is a continuous process and impacts on many other e-learning skills because it can:

- help reduce your stress, since you have fewer crises due to a lack of foresight;
- contribute to your time management;
- make you realise the issues for which you need to take responsibility;

- make you aware of when assessments are due;
- give you adequate time to resolve difficulties and problems;
- provide you with sufficient time to reflect on your learning;
- help motivate you by making the learning process smoother.

Planning should be at the heart of your e-learning skills.

Activity   Plan your revision

Revision for an assessment requires careful planning. Consider, in the context of your own e-learning course, what you need to do in order to be prepared for an examination.

Discussion

There are many ways of planning your revision. Some of the issues you should consider are:

1. The overall timetable for the course. When are the assessments and how much time will you have available for revision?
2. Preparation for revision needs to start at the beginning of the course. Your notes are partially aimed at providing you with a set of explanations suitable for revision months later. Plan time for checking your initial notes in order to annotate and fill in any gaps.
3. Do not expect too much of yourself – give yourself breaks and plenty of time.
4. What methods you employ during revision (e.g. completing past examination papers, editing your notes, reading etc.) – make the process interesting; if you are bored then you will find it difficult to revise effectively.
5. Reflect on your planning and identify what went well and what you would want to change next time.

Planning is a key activity but all plans need to be flexible and can be improved.

Activity   Planning a research project

In the context of your own e-learning course, consider how you would plan a research project. If your course does not include a project then plan another aspect of the work such as an assignment.

Discussion

One approach to planning a project is:

1. Consider the aim of the project. Some colleges will provide guidelines if the project is a major part of the course (e.g. final year project).

➜

Activity Planning a research project – *continued*

2. How much time is recommended by the college for the project? When do you need to begin? What part in the overall assessment of the e-learning course is played by the research? How is the research marked? You need to be well informed to plan effectively.
3. Identify your aims and objectives – what do you hope to achieve? Is it realistic?
4. How will you undertake the research? What methods will you use?
5. What scale of literature review will you undertake?
6. Does research involve:
   – a survey?
   – interviews?
   – experiments?
   If you are going to carry out a survey then you will need to design your questions, pilot the questionnaire and revise it. All approaches will need design effort and validation.
7. Consider how long each element of the project will take and the relationship of the elements to each other (i.e. do they need to be done sequentially or can you do them in parallel?).
8. How long will it take to write the research report? You need to allow time for it to be proof read and revised.

It is often useful to produce a visual plan of the plan. An example is shown in Figure 6.2.

January–February	March	April	May–June	July	August–September
Gathering information					
	Aims and objectives				
		Methods			
			Literature review		
				Survey	
					Writing report

Figure 6.2

► Self-assessment

Activity   Involving your tutor

In all forms of learning your tutor is a vital resource. In e-learning you need to involve your tutors in judging how you are progressing. Consider how you can make use of them. Write a short list.

Discussion

There are many ways of involving your tutor. They include:

1. **Feedback** – your tutor will provide feedback on your assignments. This can take a variety of forms but is often provided as overall comments and grades combined with annotations on assignments. You need to read the feedback carefully and ask questions. If you do not fully understand, contact your tutor and ask for clarification.
2. **Questions** – you can ask your tutor for help at any time during the course. He or she can explain difficult concepts, offer advice and suggest alternative approaches to your learning.
3. **Comparison** – to assist your self-assessment, ask your tutor how your work compares with everyone else. Your grade is important but it is very helpful if you know how everyone else has done.

Activity   Involving your peers

In all forms of learning, discussing your studies with your peers is a useful resource. They can help you to assess your progress by comparing your efforts with theirs. Consider how you can make the best use of them. Write a short list.

Discussion

There are a variety of ways of involving your peers. They include:

1. Responding to your peers' questions, requests for help and generally being positive. They will hopefully help you when you ask for assistance.
2. Be open about your own assessment and suggest that everyone will benefit if there is some form of sharing of marks.
3. Suggest establishing a self-help group where everyone can pose questions, ask for support with particular topics, etc. The more you offer help, the more assistance you are likely to receive (see plagiarism section).
4. Remember that, although a message sent to a mailgroup is forwarded to all participants, you can send individual emails to your colleagues as well. This allows you to respond directly and privately to single learners.

It is likely that your college, employer or the training provider organising the e-learning programme will be encouraging mutual support so respond positively to their efforts.

Activity   Making yourself more effective

How can you make yourself more effective at assessing your own progress? Write a list of the actions you might take.

Discussion

There are a number of possibilities including:

1. **Records** – it is useful to keep a record of feedback, marks and other assessment comments so that you can identify trends and patterns.
2. **Communication** – it is important to assess informal feedback, so you need to encourage discussion with your peers and tutors. You should be proactive in encouraging an exchange of views, ideas and reflections. These will help you assess yourself against your colleagues and the standards of the tutors.
3. **Documents** – you should have read all the course information so that you are well prepared (i.e. you know the course timetable, understand the assessment criteria and rules governing the educational institution).

There are probably many more items. What did your list include?

▶ Problem solving

There are many sources of assistance for solving technical problems available on the world wide web. Many suppliers of hardware and software provide technical advice on their websites.

Activity   Contacting a technical helpline

If you found that you had a problem with your computer and you needed to contact your technical help line, perhaps as part of the supplier's warranty, how would you go about it? List the things that you would expect the support service to want from you in order to diagnose the problem.

Discussion

This is based on my own recent experience when contacting my supplier's help line:

1. You need proof that you are a customer who can call the help line. You are often supplied with a code number to show this.
2. You should have your operating system code number (i.e. the number you enter when installing the system to show it is a legal copy). You may also need it if you have to reinstall the operating system.

→

Activity   Contacting a technical helpline – *continued*

3. You will sometimes be given a recovery CD-ROM to help you reinstall your system back to its original settings. This is useful when you have a significant failure. You should not use it unless you are certain that you understand what to do.
4. Have on hand your system and software documents (e.g. guides, etc.).
5. Keep copies of your original operating system software in case you need to reinstall it. If you suspect the problem is connected with other applications, it is a good idea to have copies of them ready too.
6. You may need screwdrivers and other tools in case you are asked to open the computer to check items.
7. Have a pen and paper to hand to make notes

What other items did you have on your list? In simple terms, you need to be organised and keep your application's software and documentation in a safe place so that it is ready when things go wrong.

Activity   Suppliers' websites

Hardware, software and service suppliers (e.g. internet service suppliers) often provide many sources of assistance when you have a problem or, perhaps more importantly, help you to prevent trouble. Identify a variety of suppliers' sites and visit them to identify what assistance they provide.

Discussion

I visited suppliers of computer equipment, applications and an internet service provider. Your own experience may be different due to the dynamic nature of the world wide web and the different suppliers. I visited the sites for Apple, Microsoft and Demon, respectively. The sites offered a wide variety of information and services such as:

1. technical information about equipment, applications and connectivity (e.g. different broadband connections);
2. access to software which you can download – this is often new versions of applications (e.g. email editors and browsers), extensions to existing products or fixes for technical problems (often called patches);
3. news about viruses or other important issues;
4. information about local suppliers, sources of help and new developments;
5. many other items.

All their sites offered comprehensive assistance for uses that should assist you with solving or preventing problems. What did you discover?

Activity   Buying software

Select a new application that you would like to buy, if you had sufficient funds (e.g. upgrade your office applications, change operating systems or buy a programming language to help you learn how to programme). Identify all the factors that you would need to consider when buying your chosen application for your computer. Many software suppliers offer special deals for students and teachers, so investigate whether you can get an educational discount. If you are sponsored by your employer, they may well have rules about the purchase of hardware and software (e.g. central purchase or loaning you equipment for the duration of the course). Write a description of the process to ensure you purchase a suitable package.

Discussion

It is important to approach the task systematically – identifying the basic information you need and then considering more complex matters. Some possible questions that you will need to answer are:

1. What is the specification of your computer system (e.g. processor, random access memory (RAM), storage capacity, CD-ROM drive, etc.)?
2. What are the recommended requirements for your new application?
3. What is the cost of the new application?
4. Do you need the full version of the application or can you use an upgrade because you have an earlier version of the software?
5. Are there any discounts for buying online? Can you download the application? Do you have to pay a delivery charge?
6. How do you install the application?
7. What users' reviews are available? Some suppliers of applications provide users' reviews of their products.

Your own list may be different, but the key to solving problems is to approach the task analytically and thoroughly.

▶ Coping with stress

Stress is part of everyone's life and it is vital that you ensure that your approach to learning minimises its influence and that you live a balanced healthy life.

Activity   Life/study balance

Previously, you considered how you spent your time over a week. This activity aims to help you improve your life/study balance. A good balance is about working smarter, rather than harder. Earlier, you monitored how you used your time to become an improved time manager. Now consider how you could reduce the pressure on yourself by working smarter. Write a list of actions.

Discussion

There are many small and large actions to help you work smarter. They include:

1. Planning and organising your time
   For example: if you are going to visit the library; consider what books or other resources you will need later in the course for future assignments and locate them alongside your immediate needs.Try to think ahead and organise yourself as early as possible.
2. Study time – everyone has preferences about when they like to carry out partic- ular tasks. Plan your work around your preferred times and be realistic about what you can achieve.
   For example: trying to write an essay after a 12-hour working day is unlikely to be successful.
3. Waste – effort is sometimes wasted by a lack of personal preparation.
   For example: you start an assignment and then realise that you have forgotten to bring a key book with you. Plan ahead and prepare yourself to make the most of your time.
4. Priorities – consider carefully what you have to do and list tasks in order of importance and urgency. 'To do' lists are a good way to prioritise actions as well as ensuring you do not forget them.

What items does your own list contain?

Activity   Healthy life

A healthy lifestyle is likely to help you control your study and life pressures. Write a list of what you feel would constitute a healthy lifestyle.

Discussion

I believe that a healthy lifestyle includes:

1. **A balanced diet** – it is important to ensure you have a healthy diet. This is likely to include five portions of fruit and vegetables everyday and minimising the consumption of saturated fats (see, e.g., www.healthspace.nhs.uk/).
2. **Regular exercise** – to keep generally fit requires that you regularly undertake short spells of exercise (i.e. 20 or 30 minutes) that leave you slightly out of breath. I like to walk briskly for 30 minutes each day. I find walking an excellent way to relax after a busy day.

→

Activity   Healthy life – *continued*

3. **Sleep** – a regular pattern of sufficient sleep is important to help you study.
4. **Reduce anxiety** – adjust your study pattern to reduce or ideally to remove stress. Time pressure is often a major part of study stress so start your work as early as possible and plan how to undertake it. Do not be a source of your own time problems – organise yourself.
5. **Support** – seek help and assistance from your tutors, peers and family. This will help to put your problems into perspective, solve them or at latest reduce their intensity.

What items does your own list contain?

► Motivation

People are motivated by many different things, but one factor that encourages most people is success. Success brings rewards such as a more interesting career, higher pay or increased self-esteem.

Activity   Success

What do you want to achieve with your life and career? What motivates you to study or work hard? Write a list of items.

Discussion

There are many things that motivate people and these are often related to personal preferences and experience but some that are common to many of us are:

1. **Self-esteem** – you feel that you are successful. Your colleagues, friends and family have a high regard for you. This often is the result of personal success with your education.
2. **Enjoying your life** – having a good time is important to many people and success with your studies can give you the freedom to relax.
3. **Confidence** – many people seek to have a personal sense of self-worth which again is an outcome of success
4. **High earnings** – many people are motivated by the possibility of earning large salaries which are possible if you are able to achieve academic success.
5. **Security** – educational achievement can result in developing a career that will ensure that financial accomplishment is one outcome.
6. **Personal achievement** – some people are motivated by the possibility of self-improvement.

What motivates you?

▶ **Reflection**

A useful way to develop your reflection skills is to keep a learning diary. This will help you to consider your learning in a systematic and ordered way. You will be able to compare and contrast each experience, your own behaviour and how you could improve your performance in the future.

A learning diary can take a variety of forms and it is more important that you reflect on its contents than how it is structured. It can simply be a calendar diary where, each day, you record your experiences and what you learned from them or you could develop a more complex structure. You might begin by considering your past experiences of the subjects being studied and your personal strengths and weaknesses in relation to them. You might list each strength and weakness, the components that make them up and actions to improve the situation.

Example:	**Writing**	
Weakness	1. Spelling – I make simple errors	– my ideas flow too fast for me to write them down, so I make mistakes
	2. Grammar – I make simple errors	– partially I am thinking too quickly, but also I do not understand some of the rules of grammar

Action

- I will spell check everything I write and ask John if he will read the more important pieces and explain what is wrong with the grammar so that I can learn the rules.

Activity Keep a learning diary

To help reflect on your own learning and experience, keep a diary of what you have learnt and the experience of learning. Establish a learning diary and keep a daily record for three or four weeks. Consider your experiences both during and at the end of the period. What do you need to change to maintain a useful learning diary and continue your records?

Discussion

Keeping a learning diary is a very personal activity and students record different aspects of their experience. I like to make a daily note of:

1. What I have done.
2. How I felt the experience helped me and why.
3. How long I spent on each part of the tasks.
4. What I leart about learning and studying from the experience.
5. What I need to improve.

I have used a variety of ways to maintain records, such as a standard diary with one page for each day, a loose-leaf folder, a word processed document and Microsoft Outlook's diary. It does not matter what method you employ, it is the process of keeping the diary that helps. Figure 6.3 shows an example daily sheet.

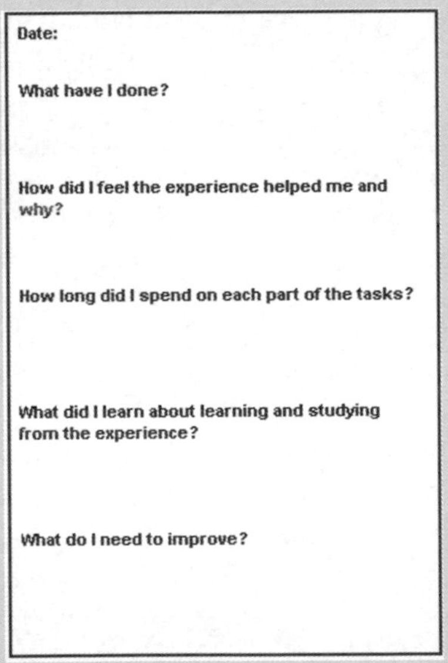
Date:

What have I done?

How did I feel the experience helped me and why?

How long did I spend on each part of the tasks?

What did I learn about learning and studying from the experience?

What do I need to improve?

Figure 6.3 Learning diary

What did you discover about your own learning and the experience of keeping a diary?

Activity   Reflecting on learning skills

You have probably had considerable experience of learning in different situations and using a variety of methods. Consider your experience of traditional forms of learning such as the lecture, tutorial, relationships with your classmates and using a library. Reflect on this experience and try to identify what experience, skills and knowledge would be most useful in an e-learning course.

Discussion

Some experience from traditional forms of learning that might be useful in e-learning are:

- **Lectures** – note taking is a useful learning skill in all types of studying, especially the ability to annotate them from independent study.
- **Tutorial** – asking questions to clarify your understanding and listening to the answers to other learners' questions are useful if they can be transferred to an e-learning environment (e.g. via email communication).
- **Relationships** – all forms of learning are enhanced by the support of other learners, so being a team player who is willing to contribute to the benefit of everyone is a positive skill.
- **Reading** – reading is a part of all courses and for e-learning an ability to browse quickly to locate key points is vital.
- **Revision** – planning your studies is a useful skill in all forms of learning and particularly in e-learning, because you have more responsibility for your own studies and freedom to choose when you learn.
- **Library** – the experience of finding books and journals may well transfer to searching for information on the world wide web.

What experience did you identify that would be useful in e-learning?

▶ Research skills

A significant area for any learner is the ability to locate and analyse information. This is often called research and it comprises a fundamental set of skills for any student or trainee. All subjects and careers require the capacity to investigate. The world wide web provides an astonishing information resource.

Activity   Research: blended e-learning methods

Consider how you would learn more about the use of blended e-learning approaches. You may search the world wide web, visit a library or both.

Discussion

My initial step was to search the world wide web using the term 'blended e-learning'. The Google search engine identified 1570 pages. Visiting some of the top 20 pages produced several definitions of blended e-learning all of which were broadly similar – blended e-learning being a combination of e-learning or online learning approaches with traditional/face-to-face methods. The pages suggested that:

1. integrating the different methods was the key factor;
2. online learning is referred to on many pages rather than e-learning, so is there a difference?
3. other terms used include web-based methods, courseware, collaboration software and EPSS.

This initial search indicates the importance of defining terms and understanding what the differences are between them. It provides information to allow you to undertake a variety of other searches. What did you discover?

Activity   Research: student retention in online learning courses

Consider how you would learn more about student retention in online learning courses. You may search the world wide web, visit a library or both.

Discussion

My initial step was to search the world wide web using the term 'online learning'. The Google search engine identified 799 000 pages. My second step was to search within these results using the term 'retention' which resulted in 16 100 pages being identified. Considering the information on the top 20 pages provided an insight into retention. It showed that I needed to consider:

1. tutors' role in retaining students;
2. learner support;
3. learner motivation;
4. learners' study skills.

These factors would allow me to undertake a series of searches and reviews of content to gain a detailed understanding of the topic.
    What did you discover?

▶ Continuous development

e-Learning comprises a new set of approaches and few people would claim that their skills do not need to improve, develop or be enhanced. It is, therefore, important to take a long-term approach to your e-learning skills and try to adopt a continuous improvement strategy to developing them. The following activity asks you to judge your current level of skill and identify opportunities for improvement.

Activity   Online learning skills assessment

Table 6.1 provides a structure for you to assess your current level of skill, what future level you would like to achieve and what opportunities you aim to take in order to develop your skills.

Table 6.1   Online learning skills assessment

Skill	Current skill level	Opportunities to develop skill
Time management 1. Achieving deadlines 2. Balancing different priorities 3. Personal organisation 4. Looking forward		
Acceptance of responsibility 1. Understanding of course structure and standards 2. Personal objectives and standards		
Planning 1. Setting goals 2. Producing action plan		

➔

Activity   Online learning skills assessment – *continued*

Table 6.1   Online learning skills assessment – *continued*

Skill	Current skill level	Opportunities to develop skill
3. Monitoring performance		
4. Adjusting plans		
Self-assessment		
1. Identifying strengths and weaknesses		
2. Reflecting on feedback		
Problem solving		
1. Identify real problem (i.e. not the symptoms)		
2. Systematic approach to solving problems		
3. Review solution and learn from experience		
Coping with stress		
1. Awareness of causes		
2. Study and life balance		
3. Reducing pressure		
Motivation		
1. Recognising personal motivation		
2. Setting objectives		
Reflection		
1. Analyse e-learning experience		

➜

Activity   Online learning skills assessment – *continued*

Table 6.1   Online learning skills assessment – *continued*

Skill	Current skill level	Opportunities to develop skill
2. Comparing different approaches/experiences		
Research		

Discussion

An example analysis of a learner's e-learning skills is shown in Table 6.2 and is intended to provide you with a comparison.

Table 6.2   Personalised online learning skills assessment

Skill	Current skill level	Opportunities to develop skill
Time management		
1. Achieving deadlines	Usually meet deadlines but a clear tendency to try to do too much.	I will draw up a personal study timetable.
2. Balancing different priorities		
3. Personal organisation	Normally looks ahead to check for deadlines.	
4. Looking forward		
Acceptance of responsibility		
1. Understanding of course structure and standards	I read the study guide at the start of the course.	I will make a poster of the course timetable for my room to remind me about deadlines.
2. Personal objectives and standards	I normally do not set myself formal objectives or consider personal standards. I simply aim to pass the assessment.	I will set distinct standards for my work and will monitor my achievements.

→

Activity Online learning skills assessment – *continued*

Table 6.1   Online learning skills assessment – *continued*

Skill	Current skill level	Opportunities to develop skill
Planning 1. Setting goals 2. Producing action plan 3. Monitoring performance 4. Adjusting plans	I tend to react to pressure and often do not plan my studies.	I will look ahead and plan my learning so that there are no crises. I will keep records of my work.
Self-assessment 1. Identifying strengths and weaknesses 2. Reflecting on feedback	At the moment I only consider the marks and rarely study the feedback.	I will carefully read comments and ask my tutor to clarify what I need to do to improve my performance. I will try to consider my performance systematically.
Problem solving 1. Identify real problem (i.e. not the symptoms) 2. Systematic approach to solving problem 3. Review solution and learn from experience	I haphazardly solve problems as I encounter them. I only occasionally review what has happened.	I will focus on learning from the software problems that I encounter by using textbooks, college helpline and supplier websites. I will keep records of what were the best approaches.
Coping with stress 1. Awareness of causes 2. Study and life balance 3. Reducing pressure	I am sometimes anxious about my course.	I will review what makes me anxious and in addition I will consider my study pattern.

→

Activity   Online learning skills assessment – *continued*

Table 6.1   Online learning skills assessment – *continued*

Skill	Current skill level	Opportunities to develop skill
Motivation 1. Recognising personal motivation 2. Setting objectives	I rarely consider my long-term motives.	I will write a list of reasons for wanting to be successful and stick them on the wall by my desk to remind me when problems are encountered.
Reflection 1. Analyse e-learning experience 2. Comparing different approaches/experiences	Although I think about the course, this is in a relatively unsystematic way.	I will keep a learning diary of how I feel and what I experience. I will attempt to write down my feelings each day as well as record what I have done.
Research	I have little experience of research.	I will seek to apply a systematic planned approach to my investigations.

It is a good practice to plan to improve your skills and you should regularly review your progress.

7 Communication Skills

Many e-learning programmes are based around the use of communication technologies and e-learners' success depends to a large extent on well-developed communication skills. This chapter will concentrate on:

- acceptable use;
- asynchronous communication;
- email communication styles;
- mailgroups and newsgroups;
- threaded discussions;
- 'lurking';
- synchronous communication;
- chat;
- audio conferencing;
- video conferencing.

A range of activities will be used to help develop your skills and understanding.

▶ Acceptable use

When you use the computer system in your college, learning centre or other public facility, it will be governed by their acceptable use policy. This is essentially a set of conditions or rules that limit the use of the computer systems. Each location will have a different policy depending on its nature, so it is important to check what you can do and the consequences of breaking the rules. Some centres and colleges may stop you using their facilities altogether if you are in breach of the rules. Some general conditions that you may encounter are to forbid you to:

- access pornographic or other offensive websites;
- download offensive material.

These are easy to understand, but others are perhaps more difficult:

- not to use personal floppy disks from your home;
- not to download software from websites.

Both of these conditions are related to the risk of infecting the system with viruses. Many viruses are transmitted across the internet or by moving files between computers without checking them for virus infection. Other conditions may forbid you downloading copyrighted materials (e.g. software applications and music) and limiting the size of files that you can download.

It is quite common for college or public systems to limit the amount of time individuals may use a computer. Facilities are often in demand and you may need to book a time to use them.

Filtering

Filtering is essentially an automated way of enforcing the acceptable use policy. Software filtering systems allow the college or centre to limit what can be accessed and downloaded from the Internet. However, some systems are relatively unsophisticated, so they may block many useful sites if they contain a word or phrase that has been used to identify forbidden websites or resources.

Other factors

There are numerous other factors to consider when using communication technologies and we discuss four of them in more detail below.

Cultural differences

Online learning removes the geographical barriers that separate learners, meaning that you can study with learners from many other cultures. This is an excellent opportunity to access a wide range of different perspectives and experiences. However, to take full advantage of this you must be willing to be tolerant of views different from your own. You can gain valuable new insights into a topic if ideas are explored rather than dismissed simply because they are different from your own. Reflect on the comments of your fellow learners and ask questions in order to develop common points of reference.

'Blogging'

'Blogging' is essentially keeping an open diary or journal of your thoughts, ideas and experiences on a website. It has been described in many ways and certainly serves many different purposes. These can be very personal in that the bloggers are revealing their own views and feelings to the world. It is similar to issuing a personal newsletter about your life. Some writers use their sites to comment on major developments, personal interests or the society in which they live.

Libel

Email and other forms of online communication sometimes make people feel they are free to say anything in any way. The reality is that, like any other form of communication, you are governed by the law. You must write with the same care that you use in more traditional communication forms.

Many organisations now add to all their emails a standard disclaimer to try and reduce the risk of offending people or breaking the laws of libel and defamation.

Privacy and security

Many people are concerned that everything they store on a computer or send by email can be intercepted or accessed by other people. In principle this is probably true but it does assume that someone would take the trouble of identifying your message or can gain access to your computer. There are several steps that you can take to protect your messages and system. These include the following.

- Securing your home to prevent easy access to your computer. You may also want to install security devices to stop the removal of your computer by using metal cables or other methods to fix the machine to a desk.
- Encrypting your files so that no one else can read them. This is very effective when you want to send confidential information by email or store sensitive data on your system.
- Password protecting your system is a straightforward and easy way of limiting access to your system. A good password is one that is very difficult to guess (e.g. a mixture of letters and numbers) and you should regularly change it.
- Using firewalls – this is an application that stops hackers gaining access to your system.

▶ Asynchronous communication

Asynchronous communication methods such as email are probably the main ones used online. They are very convenient in that:

- the sender and the recipient do not need to be available at the same time;
- you can send a message to a large number of people at the same time;
- you can add an attachment to the message (e.g. a picture, word-processing file or spreadsheet);
- you can choose when to read messages;
- you can reply to all or a selection of the people who were sent the original message;
- you can forward the original message to other people;
- you can save the messages;
- your replies can include the original message, thus containing a complete record of the communication.

In many learning programmes you will be involved in communicating with a number of other learners using email. The way people read and send messages form complex patterns. Readers exhibit widely different behaviours:

- some people will read their email messages every day or even many times a day;
- some people read their emails in batches;
- some people will be taking part in several mailgroups/conferences at the same time so will perhaps be receiving hundreds of emails everyday;
- some people will forward messages from other groups;
- some people will reply to every message, while others will very rarely reply.

These differences in behaviour often result in topics being relaunched after an interval because some participants have not read the original messages until a week or two after they were sent. Topics tend to get intertwined and several discussions are often mixed together. This makes the sequence of messages complex.

Activity   Discussion list

With two or more people, select a topic and discuss it using only short written notes. The notes should be limited to 50 words and, as each person completes a note, it should be placed in a central location so that everyone can read them when they want to.
    What happens? What method does each participant adopt?

Discussion

You may find that:

1. Each person adopts a different approach to reading and sending messages, so that his or her responses are out of sequence with everyone else.
2. It is difficult to predict what the next message will be or the order of the communications.
3. You miss the other aspects of human communication (e.g. body language, emphasis and hearing messages in sequence).

▶ Email communication styles

Email provides considerable freedom in the selection of how you would like to communicate. All communication methods have strengths and weaknesses and so far we have tended to consider the benefits of email, but one clear negative aspect is the risk of offending people. Perhaps due to the short and informal way many people write emails, it is relatively easy to offend the recipients of the messages. This is probably increased by the speed and ease of sending email, which does not encourage people to reflect on their comments and thereby realise they are being too aggressive. Netiquette was developed to combat this possibility by encouraging people to adopt rules of behaviour. A simple but useful rule is to never reply to any email in anger. You will almost certainly provoke an argument if you do.

    The key to producing a clear, polite email is to:

- address your email to the person – you can simply give the person's name, use 'Dear' or a similar phrase such as 'Hello';
- try never to be offensive;
- remember humour is difficult to communicate and can be easily misunderstood;
- use blank spaces or punctuation to make your communication clear – no punctuation may seem informal but it does not aid clarity;

- end your message with your name or closing phrase such as 'best wishes', 'many thanks' or something similar.

Figure 7.1 shows two ways of presenting an email. You may say that you would never be so blunt, but I have seen far worse.

Alternative 1

Dear John

I would be grateful if I could borrow your notes on the South Sea Bubble. They will be very useful in helping me to complete my essay.

Many thanks

Alan

Alternative 2

Send me your South Sea Bubble notes. I need them.

Figure 7.1 Email politeness

A second weakness is that the informal nature of email encourages you to write in a casual and non-grammatical way. This is often seen as friendly, but it also sometimes clouds the meaning. The presence of the original message is an encouragement to reply by annotating the sender's message and this is very useful on occasions. If you are working on a joint statement, annotations will be very useful but remember that embedding your answer in the original text may not make it easy for the reader to understand your points. The originator may not read the annotated reply for some days, by which time their memory of the original message has faded. When you insert comments into the original message, they are sometimes displayed in a different colour, but of course this distinction will disappear if the email is printed on a monochrome printer. Some email users routinely print out their communications.

The key to annotating an email is to focus on making yourself clear and your comments understandable. Some simple steps to follow to achieve these aims are:

- use blank lines to separate out your comments and the original text they relate to;
- introduce your message;
- add a short summary to conclude your message.

Figure 7.2 compares an annotated and a sequential response to the same original message. Both are intended to be effective messages, but it is probably easier to see from the annotated message that the reply does not cover all the points made in the original message. A key part of the original message was 'but with evidence that we each contributed to a group investigation'. This is important to the students since they are going to be assessed on their work together and need to provide evidence of what they did. When you are replying to a message, an annotated approach is a straightforward way to check that you are answering each point, since the original message is part of the reply.

The presentation of a response is important to avoid confusion and to communicate clearly. Figure 7.3 shows the same response as in Figure 7.2 but with the layout removed. Do you think it is as clear? In practice, the colour coding of the original and reply messages can be changed, sometimes making them indistinguishable.

It is not a matter of which response is best. Both can be useful if used in an effective way. Concentrate on making your messages clear and ensure that you are understood.

Email signatures

Many email systems allow you to establish a standard signature at the end of your messages. This can simply be your name or a short message. People use the signature function for a variety of purposes including advertising, disclaimers and humour. However, be careful since these may cause offence.

▶ Mailgroups and newsgroups

Mailgroups and newsgroups are communities of interest; if you are a member of one you will have access to information about the subject on which it is based. You can send messages to either individuals or all members of the group. The difference between the two types of group is that the emails are sent to you if you join a mailgroup, whereas you have to visit the newsgroup to receive those messages. There are

Activity   Newsgroups

Visit the Google search engine and select the Groups option to reveal a list of Usenet discussion groups. Select a subject and explore some of the groups within it. You will be able to search the group for messages and to send one of your own if you want.

Discussion

You should have found that there are many groups to select from and that you can search to find messages relating to a particular aspect of the topic. You may see a link called a 'thread'. If you click on a thread then you will be linked to the start of the discussion (i.e. when the debate or topic was raised). If you come to an interesting message you may well want to see how the discussion reached that point. Clicking on thread is the way to find out.

newsgroups and mailgroups covering almost every topic. Online courses often have specific associated mailgroups for registered students, but in some cases you can gain valuable information by being a member of a general group.

You need to subscribe to a group in order to take part, normally requiring your email address and your user name, although frequently people enrol under a pen name. Many newsgroups are known as usenet. Their names tell you in broad terms what they cover:

- Alt – alternative (as the name suggests these are alternative views. You may find offensive material but they cover an enormous range of subjects);
- Biz – business;
- Comp – computer;
- Sci – science;
- Soc – social;
- Talk – discussions about almost any topic;
- News – newsgroups;
- Rec – recreation;
- Misc – miscellaneous.

Educational organisations will filter messages to remove offensive items from their network. In some cases this will mean that whole types of usenet newsgroups will not be allowed.

Original message

Hi everyone

We need to form a group to investigate the nature of the digital divide. The course study guide suggests that we need to consider: 1. Is there a real divide in society? 2. If a divide exists is it the equivalent of other social and economic divisions? 3. What are the key features of the digital divide? 4. What would we do to close the divide or at least stop it getting any larger? We have two months to address the questions and we all need to submit an individual essay with our own response but with evidence that we each contributed to a group investigation. That seems a bit of a contradiction. We also have to say what we thought of the process of working together – I am unsure what that would involve. What does everyone think we should do – we need to get started quickly since two months is not long if we have to work together on this.

Cheers

Janet

Annotated reply

[Text in this type is the original message; *italic text is annotation.*]

Hi All

Here are some thoughts

Hi everyone

We need to form a group to investigate the nature of the digital divide.

I think we can form several small groups if we want to – there are 26 students on the course. That is too large to be a single group – why don't we divide into the groups that we had earlier for the learning object exercise?

The course study guide suggests that we need to consider:

1. Is there a real divide in society?
2. If a divide exists is it the equivalent of other social and economic divisions?
3. What are the key features of the digital divide?
4. What would we do to close the divide or at least stop it getting any larger?

Again I would divide up the different objectives so we can get the most work done.

➜

We have two months to address the questions and we all need to submit an individual essay with our own response but with evidence that we each contributed to a group investigation. That seems a bit of a contradiction. We also have to say what we thought of the process of working together – I am unsure what that would involve.

We should share all the evidence we located but then write our individual essays.

What does everyone think we should do – we need to get started quickly since two months is not long if we have to work together on this.

Can we have a quick vote on what to do – sort out who does what and get going.

Cheers

Janet

I hope these comments help

Best wishes

Linda

Simple reply

Hi All

Here are some thoughts

I think we should form several small groups – there are 26 students on the course. That is too large to be a single group – why don't we divide into the groups that we had earlier for the learning object exercise? Then divide up the different objectives amongst the group so we can get the most work done.

We can share all the evidence we find before we write our own essays.

Can we have a quick vote on what to do – sort out who does what and get going?

I hope these comments help

Best wishes

Linda

Figure 7.2   Annotation – 1

Hi All

Here are some thoughts

Hi everyone

We need to form a group to investigate the nature of the digital divide. *I think we can form several small groups if we want to – there are 26 students on the course. That is too large to be a single group – why don't we divide into the groups that we had earlier for the learning object exercise?* The course study guide suggests that we need to consider. 1. Is there a real divide in society? 2. If a divide exists is it the equivalent of other social and economic divisions? 3. What are the key features of the digital divide? 4. What would we do to close the divide or at least stop it getting any larger? *Again I would divide up the different objectives so we can get the most work done.* We have two months to address the questions and we all need to submit an individual essay with our own response but with evidence that we each contributed to a group investigation. That seems a bit of a contradiction. We also have to say what we thought of the process of working together – I am unsure what that would involve. *We should share all the evidence we located but then write our individual essays.* What does everyone think we should do – we need to get started quickly since two months is not long if we have to work together on this. *Can we have a quick vote on what to do – sort out who does what and get going.*

Cheers

Janet

I hope these comments help

Best wishes

Linda

Figure 7.3 Annotation – 2

▶ Registration

In order to join most mailgroups you need to register. You will often be required to send an email to a central address or visit the group website in order to join. This is a fairly simple process of identifying yourself in some way depending on the nature of the group. It will normally involve giving an email address so that messages can be sent to you. Often, you will need to wait for the mailgroup to send you an email with the induction materials which will explain how to send messages (e.g. email address), the conditions of participation (e.g. netiquette) and how to end your membership. This can be helpful since, until you begin to receive mailgroup messages, you are never completely sure if it is going to be useful. You should keep the mailgroup user instructions safe so you can communicate to the mailgroup administrator, end your membership or simply help others to join.

Large organisations (e.g. employers, universities and colleges) often restrict access to their online facilities to registered students, but also prevent students accessing general mailgroups or newsgroups from their systems.

▶ Moderation

Many newsgroups and mailgroups are moderated, that is, your messages are read by the moderator who decides if they should be posted. Educational moderators often have a wider role in that they will contribute to discussions, answer questions about the course, referee behaviour (e.g. stop arguments that breach the netiquette conditions) and suggest topics. They are essentially acting as facilitators to help learners gain the most from the discussion. An effective moderator does not prevent debate, but assists participants by ensuring a fair exchange of ideas.

▶ Organisation

Email systems provide you with some features to organise your emails. Mailgroups often send you large numbers of messages and, if you are a member of several, it can be difficult to cope with the volume. When you are receiving large numbers of messages, it is often a problem to identify what is important. Microsoft Outlook allows you to:

- segregate email into different folders so that you can separate out email from a particular mailgroup from other messages;
- automatically copy all messages you receive;
- remove spam email messages;
- colour code messages to help you identify different types.

These features are accessed through the Outlook Rules Wizard and the Organise Tool.

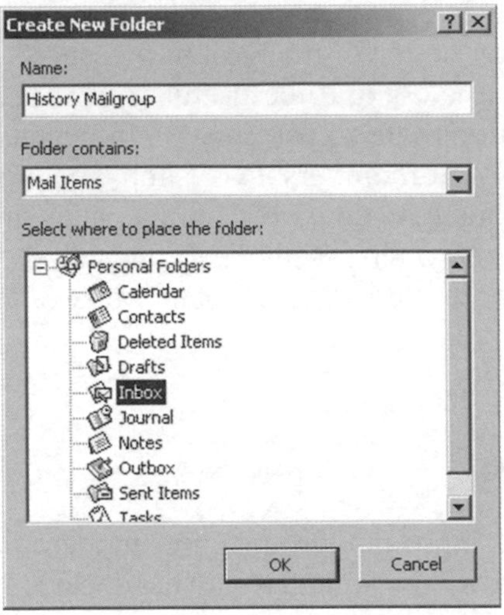

Figure 7.4 New folder

New folders

The most straightforward step to organising your emails is to create new folders in which to store your messages from mailgroups, people or those relating to different subjects. To create a new folder select the File menu, highlight the Folder option to reveal a submenu and click on the New Folder option to open the Create New Folder window (Figure 7.4). This allows you to create a new folder and position it. It is often useful to create a series of folders within the inbox folder in order to keep all messages together in a single master folder. Figure 7.5 shows that a folder called History Folder has been created within the Inbox folder.

Organizer

After creating new folders, the next step is use Outlook's Organizer feature to send messages automatically to them so that your inbox is not crowded. One way of directing messages to particular folders is to click on the Organizer button on the standard toolbar. This will open the Ways to Organize Inbox window (Figure 7.7). The current message in the inbox acts as an example of the type of messages that you want to move into the selected folder, in this example the History Folder. When you are content with the choices you click on the Create button to establish the rule.

Figure 7.5 History folder

Activity   Create new folders

Create three new folders called History Mailgroup, Tutor Messages and Student Mailgroup within your inbox folder.

Discussion

Figure 7.6 illustrates my outcome. Your own should be similar.

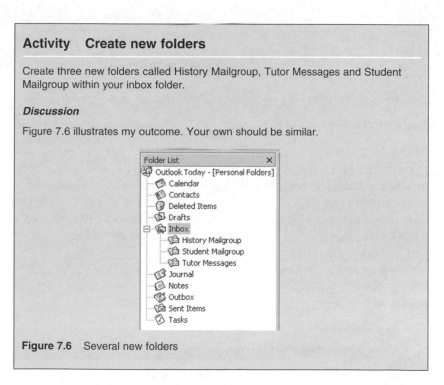

Figure 7.6   Several new folders

You can also create new folders from the Ways to Organize Inbox by clicking on the New Folder button in the top right-hand corner of the window. This will then open the Create New Folder window (Figure 7.4).

In the Ways to Organize Inbox is an option on the left-hand side of

Figure 7.7   Organize

the window called Using Colors which, if you select it, will colour code messages using the current one displayed as an example of the type you want to code (Figure 7.8). You can change the colours using the drop down list in the colour box, making it is easy to identify different types of message (e.g. all messages from your tutor are coloured red so you can immediately identify them).

A further option in the Ways to Organize Inbox is Using Views which, if you select it, will allow you to change the way your messages are displayed.

Figure 7.8   Color code

Activity   Ways to Organize Inbox

Explore the different options within the Ways to Organize Inbox to move messages to different folders, colour code different types of messages and change the display of your messages. The version of Microsoft Outlook you have will to some extent vary the options available and how they are presented.

Discussion

In my version of Microsoft Office XP, I am able to:

1. move messages to chosen folders;
2. colour code messages from certain senders;
3. change the way the inbox is presented.

What did you find?

Rules Wizard

Microsoft Outlook contains a Rules Wizard that lets you establish rules for handling your email. You can establish rules to:

- send all messages relating to a particular issue or from a particular address to a folder automatically. This allows you to segregate your messages (e.g. so that you can keep your communications from your tutor);
- delete messages from particular addresses (e.g. spam).

The wizard helps you to organise your messages.

▶ Threaded discussion

In many mailgroups, newsgroups and other forms of online dialogue the debate is shown as a threaded discussion or you will have the option of presenting the messages in this way. A threaded presentation shows you the sequences and relationships between messages. In Figure 7.9 you can see two threads. The initial message provoked three responses. Two of these motivated people to reply to them and so on. There are therefore two threads of discussion which are shown in the figure by being enclosed in a box.

It is possible to present these messages as a linear list without showing the relationship. The list is simply shown in date order, although email systems (e.g. Microsoft Outlook) frequently provide you

---

Activity   Threaded discussion

Consider your email editor and see if you can change the display of messages to present a threaded view of them. The View menu item often contains options for presenting messages as a list or as a thread.

Explore the threaded messages and reflect on what the benefits of this type of display are.

Discussion

To a large extent your experience will depend on the email editor you are using. However, if you have never considered a threaded display before, then at first it may not be obvious what the benefit is. You will probably be influenced by how different it is to a list display. Changing a familiar presentation is uncomfortable for most people.

The major benefit is that you can quickly identify the relationships between different emails, which message initiated the discussion (thread) and how the messages relate to each other. This is important if you are trying to gain an insight into a new issue or to remind yourself of an argument. It is very useful if you check the emails after an interval, as the order in which you read them may influence your understanding or alternatively confuse you. The thread shows you the order of the debate and how the discussion arrived at its present point.

It can take time to fully appreciate a threaded presentation, so you may have to continue for a few days or even weeks.

What was your own experience?

---

with the choice of listing messages in other ways (e.g. unanswered). However, if you only occasionally read your messages (i.e. many emails arrive between visits) understanding the nature of the debate is more difficult. A threaded discussion makes it easier to understand the debate, but initially it can be more confusing since the presentation is more complex. If you explore a threaded discussion, you can analyse the contributions and relationships between messages. This is, potentially, a powerful aid to understanding and analysing the discussion. After a face-to-face debate, it is often difficult to remember all the points made, answered or disputed. A threaded discussion provides you with a record of the whole story.

A list presentation sometimes shows you that a message is a reply to an earlier message by changing the subject line in the email. This helps the reader to recognise a response, but does not show the whole communication relationship (i.e. thread).

Example:
Initial message   Response
Secondment opportunity   Re: Secondment opportunity

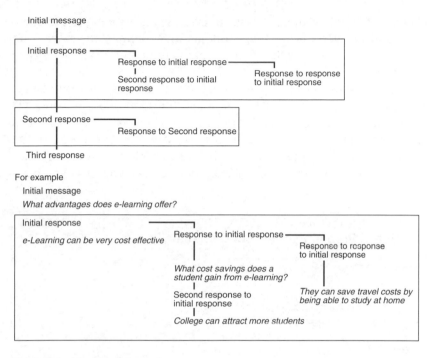

Figure 7.9 Threaded discussion

If you are only an occasional participant in a discussion group then it can take some time to catch up with the communications. However, an equivalent face-to-face debate would be almost impossible to understand if you missed a large part of the discussion. Online discussions do give you a complete record of the debate.

▶ 'Lurking'

Mailgroups and other forms of online communication groups are a key part of many e-learning programmes. They mainly operate by sharing all the messages sent by any one individual participant with everyone registered with the group. However, the behaviour of some participants has been described as 'lurking'. This essentially describes someone who rarely or never sends messages to the group. Nonnecke and Preece (2001) reported that the reasons for lurking varied and that lurking might meet individual needs if these members get what they want from the mailgroup without having to post messages. This is perhaps the equivalent of not asking questions in class, while listening to the questions and answers from other students and tutors. You do gain an insight into the subjects, but you are not getting answers to your own questions.

To ask a question in a face-to-face class requires self-confidence. There is always a fear that it is a stupid question and everyone will think that you are fool. Similar doubts occur in mailgroups but with significant differences, such as you have to write your question and can check that it is a sensible one before posting it. In a face-to-face situation, you need to speak and everyone can see you, so if you hesi-

---

Activity   Preparing contributions to mailgroups

Prepare your responses in reply to these messages:

1. What do you find most difficult about studying?
2. What have you gained most from studying?
3. How would you describe yourself?

Discussion

My own responses to these questions are:

1. What do you find most difficult about studying?

Most of my recent study (over the last fifteen years) has had to be combined with working full time. This means that I am always trying to read text books, writing essays or researching in the evening or at weekends. I always seem to be trying to fit in too many things, squeezing my family responsibilities into the gaps, struggling to meet deadlines and satisfy my employers.

2. What have you gained most from studying?

I have developed self-confidence. It has helped me to gain valuable skills such as writing for publication as well as developing an understanding of many subjects. This has helped me in my career and personal life.

3. How would you describe yourself?

I am a middle-aged man of fifty-one years with grey hair. I have been married for nearly twenty-nine years and have two adult sons. I work for a national educational charity trying to encourage people to use ICT to support and deliver learning.

If I had doubts about these messages I could ask a friend or family member to check them before posting.

tate or stumble over the words the whole class will know. In a mail-group you can present yourself in any way you like.

Some e-learning programmes assess your contribution to group activities, such as mailgroups, so you need to be able to send messages and join in the debate. If you are unsure then you should:

- prepare your messages away from the mailgroup;
- check them yourself or ask a friend to help;
- post the messages;
- respond to replies.

It is often best to send messages at an early stage in the group's formation when everyone is trying to be a part of it. Many messages have little punctuation and ignore grammatical rules, so you are unlikely to make an error that anyone will notice. Spelling mistakes are common, but can be eliminated by using the spellcheckers provided within email applications.

▶ Mailgroup digests and summaries

A useful feature of many mailgroups is that they regularly publish a digest or summary of the discussion, allowing you to follow it without the burden of reading every message. The digest is normally published at certain intervals (e.g. weekly or monthly) so you can see if the debate is appropriate to you. Mailgroups will often archive all messages so if you realise a discussion is relevant then you can seek out and consider the individual messages. Some mailgroups, however, do not publish a digest nor archive messages, so you need to read the conditions under which it operates to check which services it offers.

▶ Synchronous communication

Synchronous communication requires that all the participants are involved at the same time. A telephone conversation is synchronous since both parties have to be present. If you leave a message on an answer machine then the communication is asynchronous. There are three main online synchronous communication methods:

- chat;

- audio conferencing;
- video conferencing.

Chat

Chat lets you to communicate with one or more other people through text messages in real time. It is useful for having general discussions in that topics can be changed quickly, so helping group formation amongst new students. It is often an enjoyable experience, breaking down the barriers between students. It is less effective for considering a topic in depth. It has been used for one-to-one tutorials.

If you have never participated in a chat session, try the chat activity.

There are a variety of chat systems including:

- Internet Relay Chat;
- Webpage Chat;
- Instant Message Chat.

Internet Relay Chat (IRC) was the original form of chat, it requires you to have a chat application installed on your computer. Instant Message Chat is essentially a simplified form of Internet Relay Chat requiring the use of a message client (i.e. a message application). Webpage Chat has the advantage that you do not need an application to take part but rather you participate through your browser.

Activity   Chat

Locate some chat services on the world wide web and take part in a chat session. However, some public chatrooms can be offensive and you should never give your name or any personal details.

Discussion

I visited the Yahoo Chat room at http://chat.yahoo.com/ which offers chat sessions related to a wide range of subjects. You select by clicking on the topic you are interested in and are then asked to register. This involves giving yourself a user identification and password. Once you have registered you can take part in the chat session.

When you visit the chatroom on subsequent occasions you simply identify yourself and then you can take part. What did you do?

Audio conferencing

A critical factor in all forms of audio conference is that you cannot see the other participants. This removes the richness of non-verbal communication (e.g. knowing when the other person wants to speak, disagrees with your comments or is simply not interested). In an audio conference, an effective chairperson is crucial to organise and control the communication. This is normally a tutor but occasionally students will need to arrange their own meetings.

Often audio conferences give each participant the opportunity to speak in turn. This can take a long time if everyone has a contribution to make and tends to make the event quite formal. For you to gain the most from an audio conference you need to:

- prepare in advance what you want to say and any questions you want to ask;
- keep a record of the discussion (e.g. simple notes or an audio recording);
- concentrate on the discussion – this can be difficult when you have no visual prompts.

Activity   Audio conference preparation

You are going to take part in an audio conference to consider the priorities for supporting students using the college library. The conference is timetabled to last for an hour and will involve six participants including yourself. What would you prepare and hope to achieve?

Discussion

Most audio conferences limit what you are able to say so, even if you have an equal share of the time, you will only have 10 minutes. This will probably be made up of perhaps three contributions spread over the hour. You need to consider how to make the best use of this time.

I normally consider what my aims are for the conference (e.g. to extend the opening hours of the help desk) and keep them narrow and focused. In an audio conference, you are more likely to achieve a limited goal than an ambitious one.

I list all the points I would like to make and prioritise them. Usually other contributors make some of them for you so you can work down your list and sometimes achieve more than you thought possible. It takes very little time to say, 'I agree with . . . and would like to add . . . '

Before the conference starts, I make sure I have everything I need (e.g. preparation notes, pens, notebook etc.). How did you prepare?

Audio conferences are most useful when they concentrate on a distinct issue related to a limited topic. They allow a group of participants to reach a decision without the need to meet. Groups should not be too large otherwise the conference can become cumbersome. A reasonable rule is not to exceed six participants. In e-learning, audio conferences have effectively been used as a means of offering a tutorial to answer questions and discuss a topic.

These are not a spontaneous communication method, since ad hoc comments will confuse or distract from the central theme and often it is not easy to recognise voices. It is good practice to introduce yourself when you make a contribution and to speak clearly and concisely. You should not interrupt other participants. At the start of the event, it is sensible to agree the objectives so you should prepare in advance what you want to achieve.

The key to successful audio conferencing is preparation.

Video conferencing

Video conferences have many things in common with audio conferencing, principally they both limit the normal non-verbal communications of face-to-face communications. The quality of the video varies considerably between different systems and there are a number of ways of organising the conference such as:

- tutor remote from a group or several groups of learners;
- tutor located with a group; other remote individuals or groups of learners linked by video conference to them;
- everyone separated.

There are other permutations and combinations, meaning that the communication skills will vary depending on the structure of the conference.

Video conferencing can limit the opportunity each participant has to contribute, rather like audio conferencing,but it is not quite as restrictive in that you can see each other. The tendency to be formal and to organise contributions remains, which can make the discussion lengthy. To gain the most from a video conference you need to:

- prepare in advance what you want to say and any questions you want to ask;
- keep a record of the discussion (e.g. simple notes);
- concentrate on the discussion – this is difficult as your view of

Activity   Video conference preparation

You are going to take part in a video conference to consider how you can undertake a group assignment with other learners. The conference is timetabled to last for two hours, will involve six participants including yourself and is being chaired by your tutor. What would you prepare and hope to achieve?

Discussion

Before the conference starts, I would make sure I have everything I need and that the camera is positioned to show me. I would close the room door and try to discourage interruptions. I would also check that my dress is acceptable.

Most video conferences limit what you are able to say – even if you have an equal share of the time you will only have 20 minutes, probably made up of about three to six contributions spread over the two hours. You need to know how to make the best use of this time.

I would consider what my aims are for the conference and keep them narrow and focused. In a video conference you are more likely to achieve a limited goal than an ambitious one.

I list all the points that I would like to make and prioritise them. Usually, other contributors will make some of them for you so that you can work down your list and sometimes achieve more that you thought possible. Remember that you can use visual signals such as giving the thumbs up to show you agree. This is very similar to an audio conference, but with video it is probably easier to make your points and to gain understanding.

How did you prepare?

    participants will depend on camera quality and set up (e.g. camera angles);
- remember that sometimes people can see you even when you are not speaking;
- remember that if you move, you may not be visible but probably can be heard.

Video conferences, like audio conferences, are most useful when they concentrate on a distinct issue related to a limited topic. They allow a group of participants to reach a decision without the need to meet. Groups should not be too large as the conference will become cumbersome, but the precise number depends on the technology and structure being employed, unless a straightforward online lecture is being given. In e-learning, video conferences have been used effectively as a means of offering a tutorial to answer questions, presenting a seminar to develop a new theme or allowing a co-operative group to meet and discuss a topic.

Video conferences are not a spontaneous communication method

Activity   Online learning communication skills assessment

Table 7.1 provides a structure for you to use to assess your current level of skill and what opportunities you aim to take advantage of in order to develop your skills.

Table 7.1   Online learnig communication skills assessment

Activity	Current skill level	Opportunities to develop skill
Email		
Mailgroups		
Newsgroups		
Chat		
Audio Conferencing		
Video Conferencing		

Discussion

Table 7.2   Personalised online learning communication skills assesment

Activity	Current skill level	Opportunities to develop skill
Email	I have been using email for several years.	I have never really used a threaded system. I will change the display of my email editor to display the communication threads to learn more about this approach.
Mailgroups	Occasionally I have joined mailgroups, but I have rarely sent messages.	I will join some mailgroups that are relevant to my course and try to participate regularly in the discussion.
Newsgroups	I have only occasionally joined a newsgroup and never for very long.	I will join some relevant newsgroups and review their value over a four-week period.
Chat	I have never used a chatroom.	I will register with a chat service and take part in some sessions to explore them.
Audio conferencing	I have never taken part in an audio conference.	I will seek to participate in audio conferencing to gain an insight into this method.
Video conferencing	I have only taken part in one type of video conferencing where two groups meet through the technology.	I will seek to gain experience of other types of video conferencing especially participating at home through a low speed line.

since, to be effective, they need a large degree of organisation. It is good practice to introduce yourself when you make a contribution and to speak clearly and concisely. You should not interrupt other participants, but it is sometimes possible to add comments once they have finished and before the next formal contribution. At the start of the event, it is sensible to agree the objectives so you should prepare in advance what you want to achieve.

As with audio conferencing, the key to successful video conferencing is preparation.

► Summary

1. **Acceptable use**

   The use of public computer facilities is normally governed by an acceptable use policy which sets out the rules that control how you use the system (e.g. when, how and what you can do with the technology). Many public learning centres employ filtering software to limit your access to and use of the Internet.

2. **Some factors when using communication technologies**
   - Cultural differences – online learning removes the geographical barriers that separate learners so that you can study with learners from many other cultures.
   - Blogging – blogging is essentially keeping an open diary or journal of your thoughts, ideas and experiences on a website.
   - Libel – email and other forms of online communication are governed by the laws of libel and defamation.
   - Privacy and security – there are several steps that you can take to protect your messages and system including home security, encrypting files, using passwords and employing firewalls.

3. **Asynchronous communication**

   Email is an asynchronous communication method and probably the most widely-used one. It has many advantages in that you can send messages at any time to one or many people, with or without attachments. In a similar way, you have the freedom to read messages when it is convenient. People read and send messages in many different and complex ways.

4. **Email communication styles**

It is relatively easy to offend people unintentionally, perhaps due to the short and informal way many people write emails. This is probably increased by the speed and ease of an email message. It is important always to send polite emails and never respond to a message in anger.

Most emails are written in an informal style, which is friendly but can sometimes be difficult to understand. When replying, many people will annotate the original message. It is important to concentrate on replying in a way that is clear to your receiver.

5. **Mailgroups and newsgroups**

Mailgroups and newsgroups are communities of interest that allow you to participate in discussions about their topic. Groups cover almost all subjects (e.g. business, computing and science). You need to register with a group in order to take part – this will involve giving your name and email address. Many newsgroups and mailgroups are moderated. Moderators essentially referee the discussion although their role in education is to facilitate the debate.

6. **Organisation**

You can receive very large numbers of emails, especially if you participate in mailgroups. Microsoft Outlook and other email systems provide you with many features to organise your emails, letting you save them, segregate different types of messages, create new folders and remove spam.

7. **Threaded discussion**

In many forms of online discussion, the debate can be shown as a threaded discussion. A threaded presentation shows you the sequences and relationships between messages. This allows you to understand the relationship between the different themes being discussed.

8. **'Lurking'**

Many participants of mailgroups send very few messages. This behaviour is called lurking. This has been described as the equivalent of not asking questions in a class while listening to the questions and answers from other students and tutors.

9. **Mailgroup digests and summaries**
    Many mailgroups publish a regular digest or summary of the discussion (e.g. weekly or monthly). It allows you to maintain an interest in the discussion without having to read the many individual messages. In any public forum you should never give your name or any personal details.

10. **Synchronous communication**
    Synchronous communication requires that participants take part simultaneously. The three main online synchronous communication methods are:

    * chat;
    * audio conferencing;
    * video conferencing.

    Chat
    Chat allows you to communicate using text messages in real time rather like a conversation. It has been used to simulate the types of informal communication had by learners meeting face-to-face.

    Audio conferencing
    The critical factor in an audio conference is that you do not have the benefit of non-verbal communication clues. It is important to set up an organised and controlled event which is mainly the role of the tutor. In order to gain the most benefit from an audio conference participants need to:

    * prepare in advance;
    * keep a record of the discussion;
    * concentrate on the discussion.

    Audio conferences are most useful:

    * when they concentrate on a limited topic;
    * limit participation to a small group;
    * when they focus on agreed objectives.

    The key to successful audio conferencing is preparation.

Video conferencing

Video conferences are broadly similar to audio conferences, but are not as limited in the amount of non-verbal communication avaiable to participants. There are a wide variety of ways of organising a video conference such as:

- tutor remote from a group or several groups of learners;
- tutor located with a group; other remote individuals or groups of learners linked by video conference to them;
- everyone separated.

Communication skills will vary depending on the structure of the conference. Some general points are:

- they limit the opportunity for each participant to contribute;
- there is a tendency to be formal and highly organised.

In order to gain the most benefit from video conferencing you need to:

- prepare in advance;
- keep a record of the discussion;
- concentrate on the discussion;
- remember that sometimes people can see and hear you even when you are not contributing.

Video conferences are most useful when:

- they concentrate on a limited topic;
- they focus on decision making;
- they limit participation to a small group;
- they provide a tutorial;
- they allow a co-operative group to meet.

The key to successful video conferencing is preparation.

8 Group and Co-operative Learning

This chapter will extend and build on Chapter 7 into a consideration of group and co-operative learning. It will concentrate on:

- group working online (e.g. collaboration, contributions and organisation);
- co-operative learning;
- online seminars, discussions and conferences;
- video, audio and text conferencing;
- peer assessment.

▶ Group working online

Although e-learning is often described in terms of individualised study, a major element is group or collaborative learning. Face-to-face learning often involves group activities and there are many similarities as well as differences with e-learning. The key benefits of group learning are:

- to encourage you to compare and contrast your own views, ideas and conclusions with other learners;
- with peer support you may be more willing to ask another learner rather than your tutor about elements of the subject you do not understand;
- to motivate you to explore new and difficult areas with the additional support of the group;
- to develop new skills such as analysis, communication and assessment of evidence.

On some courses, group work will be a compulsory part of the programme while others will encourage you to form groups to consider certain problems. However, you can take the lead yourself and initiate the formation of a discussion group.

The largest difference between face-to-face and e-learning groups is immediacy. In a traditional group, you can see your partners and any comments you make get immediate feedback. An e-learning group is normally linked through email and often communication exchange takes days, then starts and stops as different group members read their messages at different times.

Traditional groups are usually quite small (i.e. six to eight people) and e-learning groups are often a similar size if they are focused on completing an assignment or project. However, if their purpose is far wider (e.g. a common interest) some e-learning groups are far larger and groups of hundreds and even thousands exist.

Group formation

All groups require time to coalesce into an effective unit, with some groups never quite forming a coherent whole. This is true of both face-to-face and e-learning groups. Face-to-face groups have the advantage

---

Activity   Email communication cycle

Send an email to a group that you belong to. It does not have to be a learning group but send a message to a large number of people (i.e. twenty or more) that asks for a response. Monitor when you receive replies.

Discussion

I sent an email to the people I work with and I received the following responses:

- First day – 1 reply
- Second day – 2 replies
- Third day – no replies
- Fouth day – no replies
- Fifth day – 3 replies
- Sixth day – 1 reply
- Seventh day – no replies
- Eighth day – 1 reply
- Ninth day – no replies
- Tenth day – no replies

Several recipients of the original email have not replied and so could potentially still respond. It is not unusual to receive responses weeks after an original message. Compare this pattern with a face-to-face meeting where you would get the feedback within a few minutes.

Activity   Reflect on the email communication cycle

Consider the difference in time scale between traditional and email communication and how it would influence the work of a group.

Discussion

There are a number of thoughts that this type of communication cycle suggested to me:

1. It is more difficult to get a quick decision, since it is complicated getting agreement with email without giving deadlines. So perhaps you need to specify a date by which responses are required. However, this does reduce some of the freedom that may have been a major motivator for people to take part in e-learning.
2. Since there is a time delay in responding to an individual comment, it is likely that several different messages/ideas will be discussed in parallel. A face-to-face group will tend to be more sequential in its discussions, although no group is ever completely linear. The leader of an e-learning group will need to be aware of the parallel discussions.
3. It is a more intricate matter leading an e-learning group, since a dispersed group is harder to influence. This is both an advantage and a disadvantage as participants cannot be easily silenced, whereas a traditional group can be dictated to by a single strong personality. Email is far harder to dominate.

of immediacy, while e-learning groups have time to think about responses, which is often beneficial. All new groups have a degree of uncertainty about them. When you are asked to join a group you should consider:

*   What is the purpose of the group (e.g. what are its aims and objectives)?
*   What is the time scale for the group (i.e. deadlines)?
*   What are you aiming to achieve (i.e. outcomes)?
*   What role do you want to play in the group?

Even students who are usually confident will approach a new group with some doubts and anxiety. It is perfectly normal for you to feel uneasy at first. Everyone does. It is important not to let this natural nervousness stop you from participating and learning from the experience. Moderators should be aware that forming a group requires time and support. They should provide the motivation by explaining the group's purpose, ensuring that everyone understands what they are aiming to do and generally encouraging progress.

Activity   Problems with group formation

You will have taken part in many groups during your education, work and other experiences. Consider your own experience of groups and identify the main problems of working in a group.

Discussion

Some of the main problems that I have encountered in e-learning groups are:

1. In all types of group, both face-to-face and e-learning, there is often disagreement between participants. This can be about almost any aspect of the group's work and it can result in the group breaking down into sub-groups or even individuals who choose to undertake the task on their own. In e-learning programmes participation in group activities is frequently assessed, so you will lose marks if you do not join in.
2. E-learning provides learners with the choice of where, when and at what pace to take part, so to take part in group activities, some degree of compromise is needed. Some learners will be unwilling or unable to change their preferred ways of working so their participation may be irregular. This can be frustrating if you are waiting for a team member to report in order to take the work forward.
3. Occasionally the group fails to complete a task. The reasons vary – perhaps it is due to arguments within the groups, too few people willing to make a contribution or simply that the task is too difficult.

Group formation will slowly start to happen with participants gradually becoming more open and willing to express their opinions. It is important that when you notice this happening you should contribute fully. Sometimes, at this point, a degree of argument creeps into the group formation. People begin to position themselves to take on particular roles. The structure of the group begins to consolidate and accepted ways of working emerge from the discussion.

This process happens in both face-to-face and e-learning groups. The major difference is that a face-to-face group may form in a few hours, while an e-learning group will usually take longer due to the nature of email and other online communication methods.

Comparing face-to-face with e-learning groups
Table 8.1 analyses and compares the operation of face-to-face and e-learning groups.

Tutor's role
In e-learning the tutor is often termed a moderator or an e-moderator. As the name suggests, the role is not that of the traditional tutor but

Activity   e-Learning group

Consider Table 8.1, which compares face-to-face and e-learning groups and also your own experience of working in a group. How would you ensure that you will gain most from the experience?

Discussion

Some of the things you might want to do are:

1. Make sure you understand what you are being asked to do and that you understand the outcome required (e.g. some group activities are assessed to judge your personal contribution and for peers to assess each other's actions).
2. Volunteer to play an active role in the group, perhaps accepting the leadership of a sub-task or even the whole group. You will learn a great deal about the subject and people by taking on responsibility for a task. If you choose to play a minimum role, you will limit what you learn from the experience.
3. e-Learning groups are not a series of meetings but a continuous process of communication so you need to organise yourself through:
    *   regularly checking your email, bulletin board or other discussion list;
    *   keeping records of the group (e.g. set up a folder to save messages and other documents);
    *   planning your involvement (e.g. research time, reflection time to consider other participant contributions).
4. Reflect on your own group role to improve your contribution.
5. Be proactively helpful to other group members without interfering.

What did you conclude?

rather as a facilitator of learning who moderates the discussion, provides advice about the objectives of the activity and acts as a resource for the group. The responsibility for the successful outcome of the group work rests with the participants. The moderator is a resource who assists learners to reach the desired outcome.

Synchronous learning

Video conferencing and other forms of synchronous e-learning sometimes take the form of a lecture to a large number of learners in varying locations, with the learners taking part in a group rather than as individuals. An expert may provide an hour-long presentation of some new development, while a large number of people listen and watch, similar to a traditional lecture. In a traditional lecture, it is possible to ask individual questions or for the lecturer to divide the audience into buzz groups to consider an issue or to decide on questions. These methods can also be used in video conferencing. Often individual learners are

Table 8.1   Comparing face-to-face with e-learning groups

Element	Face-to-face	e-Learning
Environment	The activities can be relatively short. In some cases a few minutes is given to complete a simple task. However, it can also involve complex tasks requiring many meetings over several weeks or months. Meetings take place face-to-face in a room.	Normally not suitable for short group activities and requires weeks to complete the group task. Participants are in their own homes, learning centre or other ICT access point. They often have not seen or met their group members.
Tutor's role	Facilitation, briefing and group supporter through face-to-face communication. Tutor is immediately available.	Facilitation, briefing and group support at a distance usually through email. Tutor is available after normal email delays.
Communication	Communication is spoken and includes body language. Records have to be made by taking minutes so one participant will be pre-occupied by this task. Record is likely to be partial. Communication tends to be more whole group than Individual.	Normally communication is in writing. Electronic discussion provides a means of keeping a full accurate record of the discussion without participants being distracted from the principle task. Communication tends to be more individual than whole group.
Focus	Face-to-face groups often concentrate on single issues.	e-Learning groups have the potential to consider more than a single topic. There is a danger of the group going off on tangents.
Size of group	Ideally 6 to 8 people but often larger.	Often 6 to 8 people but far larger groups can be involved although usually on less focused issues.
Relationships	Normally a single group with no outside links to other groups.	Often groups will be linked to others.

→

Table 8.1   Comparing face-to-face with e-learning groups – *continued*

Element	Face-to-face	e-Learning
Participation 1. Frequency of contribution 2. Size of contribution	The nature of the participation will be dependent on the confidence of the individual learners taking part. Dominant individuals may well influence the nature of the debate. Contributions are limited by the length of each meeting and the reaction of other members. You are more conscious of the reaction your contribution is making through non-verbal communication.	There are few barriers to participation. However, there is probably less peer pressure to join in than in a face-to-face group. Lurking or simply reading other people's messages while not contributing yourself is a common occurrence. Some educational groups assess your contribution so that you may have to participate.
Subjects 1. Introducing new subjects 2. Building on earlier contributions 3. Duration of discussion	Discussion tends to focus on a limited range of issues. Parallel discussions often fragment a face-to-face group. Building on other people's contribution depends on whether the person is influential within the group. A quiet person's views may well be lost. Building on ideas is mostly immediate. Discussions are limited by the time available for each meeting and are therefore disjointed.	Any subject can be raised at any time since everyone is free to send a message. This does tend to lead to many parallel discussions. The record of the discussion and your own choice of when to read the messages allows you to build on previous contributions whenever you want to. This does often lead to discussions restarting about issues raised days or even weeks earlier. Discussions are continuous and you are free to join in whenever it is appropriate to you.
Facilitator/ moderator	It is important to agree who will act as the group's spokesperson, record keeper and any other roles. This will ensure a record of conclusions is kept and someone takes on the role of ensuring that the task is achieved (i.e. you do not go off at a tangent).	In all groups it is important to define each person's role. It is often useful to ask someone at act as the group leader, facilitator or moderator. In many large online groups a moderator is appointed who will often act as a referee, intervening if the discussion is aggressive or breeches netiquette rules.

➜

Table 8.1   Comparing face-to-face with e-learning groups – *continued*

Element	Face-to-face	e-Learning
Records	Someone has to agree to make notes of what is agreed. These are often at best a limited record of the discussion and may miss key contributions.	The computer makes a record of all the contributions so everyone has access to a full record of the group's discussion. The full record of the discussion allows for a detailed review of the group's work to be undertaken.
Review	Any review will be based mainly on the individual memory of the participants and the limited notes taken.	
Reflection	You can reflect on any experience but in a face-to-face group your reflection will be based on your memory and is likely to be more subjective.	As a full record of your contribution is available, you can undertake detailed objective reflection that will probably help you refine your arguments and approach.
Summarising	It is useful in any discussion to produce an agreed summary that will help the group come to agreements and focus their efforts.	Moderator will often produce a summary of the discussion at intervals.
Conclusion	The leader will need to propose to the group what he or she believes are the agreed conclusions. The other group members are then free to agree, disagree or build on the suggested conclusion.	Any proposed conclusion can be considered in depth and involve everyone in the debate.

asked to write questions on cards, which are then collected and sent to the speaker by email, telephone or through another communication method. Buzz groups can also be employed to give feedback or to agree questions. In a large video conference this is slightly cumbersome but it does allow some degree of interaction. While smaller events can be more effective, the large scale approach has the significant advantage of being more cost effective and provides the opportunity for many people to hear directly from an expert.

Small synchronous groups have a great deal in common with face-

---

Activity   Preparation for a video conference

What would you need to do to prepare for a time-limited video conference?

Discussion

Video conferencing needs a more structured approach than a mailgroup. Each person is often asked to comment in turn. This means that, although a meeting may last an hour, your own participation may only last a few minutes. It is therefore important to prepare what you would like to say in a clear and concise way. If someone has already provided the comments you wanted to make then simply say so. Time is very valuable and everyone will thank you for being generous.

During a video conference you are mainly listening or occasionally asking a question. It is important to go prepared to take notes and with any papers that you need so that you can easily follow the contributions. You will only get the opportunity for an occasional question, so make sure you ask the important ones.

---

to-face ones, in that a key factor is to arrange times when everyone can meet. This is a major limitation to face-to-face group work and the added factor of access to specialist video conferencing equipment contributes to this issue. Video meetings are often limited to a fixed time, so it is essential that each participant adequately prepares for the meeting to maximise the contact time. This normally means that the meetings need to be led by one of the group and that, essentially, an agenda is followed. Although this reduces spontaneity and serendipity during the meetings, considerable progress can usually be made on the task.

There is clearly a low-cost approach to video conferencing with individual participants using their own cameras over the world wide web. This is perfectly feasible and is more flexible, but still requires fixed-time meetings. It is often used in combination with email to maximise its effectiveness.

Asynchronous learning

A major asynchronous learning method is the mailgroup. These are normally focused on a particular issue, but many e-learning courses have an overall group for the course so that students can discuss any aspect of it. There are then smaller more specialist mailgroups covering key aspects of the course. You will often be made a member of this type of group as part of enrolling on the programme.

Simply placing a group of learners into the same mailgroup does not guarantee that they will take part. In most cases, very little happens unless it is encouraged and in many courses a tutor or tutors have been appointed to moderate the group. Their role is to help break down barriers and encourage participation. Often you will be asked to introduce yourself during the early stages of the course. This usually takes the form of:

- who you are;
- what you would like to discuss;
- why you are doing the course;
- anything interesting about yourself.

In a face-to-face group the most difficult step to take is starting to speak. The same is true in a mailgroup, as everyone fears making a fool of themselves. The introduction helps to get the discussion started and will often generate questions, perhaps simply about the course structure so starting the communication process.

Sometimes the moderators will seek to initiate a debate about an issue by introducing ideas or concepts either directly or through a student who has been asked to help. These methods have a mixed rate of success. In most mailgroups, a majority of members rarely participate. This is called lurking and is often seen as negative behaviour, but reading the messages and learning from the debate is very similar to listening to questions and answers in a conventional classroom. Although you will benefit from it, you will gain more if you participate by sending messages, asking questions and offering contributions. The more you give, the more you will receive.

At an early stage the group moderator will explain the netiquette governing the communication process or ask members of the mailgroup itself to suggest conditions. This has the advantage of encouraging communication and allowing participants to agree the rules. Most people are more likely to obey rules when they have conributed to drawing them up.

Individual versus group outcomes

The outcome of e-learning group activities is often specified as an individual piece of work. That is, you are asked to work with some of your fellow students but produce your own result rather than submit a joint effort. It is important before you start a group activity to check what is expected from you. You may find that:

- An individual outcome (e.g. a personal report or essay) is expected.

Activity   Introduction to a mailgroup

You have been asked to introduce yourself to a mailgroup explaining:

1. Who you are.
2. What you would like to discuss.
3. Why you are doing the course.
4. Anything interesting about yourself.

You are starting a course to study e-learning methods. What would you say?

Discussion

This is my simple introduction. It is fairly short so that people will be encouraged to read it, yet it also includes a question that is bothering me.

My name is Alan Clarke.
   I am Interested in most of the course topics but at the moment I am not entirely sure how much flexibility I have in studying. Can I decide when I do assignments or are there fixed deadlines?
   I am doing the course as part of my employer's continuous professional development programme. We are considering using e-learning methods within the organisation.
In contrast to e-learning, I collect postcards and keep guinea pigs.

What would you say?

Activity   Contributions to mailgroups

You are a student undertaking an e-learning methods course. Write a short list of possible questions or topics that you might introduce into the course mailgroup discussion.
   Once you have written your list, consider the course you are doing or looking into, and produce another list.

Discussion

A possible list is:

1. Lurking in mailgroups – this interests me, as I often find contributing difficult but I learn a great deal from reading other people's contributions.
2. Group working – I normally prefer to work/learn on my own, so I want to find out what everyone else thinks about having to complete some group assignments.
3. Content creation – what tools have people used – what are the advantages and limitations of different tools?

What did you list?

- You will be assessed on your contribution to the group – this may take the form of either your tutor/moderator assessing your involvement or group members marking each other's work (e.g. you mark their individual contributions and they mark yours).
- A group outcome is expected.
- A combination of group or individual outcome, in addition to your contribution, forms the assessment.
- The group work is not assessed.

▶ Co-operative learning

Co-operative learning is when two or more learners work together in a co-operative way that promotes their individual learning. A co-operative learning activity, especially if the participants are at a distance and initially know little about each other, requires consideration, care and understanding of each other. Some of the factors to take into consideration for co-operating with others in e-learning are:

- Do not reply in anger, no matter how provoked you feel by an email.
- Support everyone in the group to enable them to play a part.
- Consider all contributions carefully.
- Do not dismiss an idea because you do not understand it – ask for more details.
- Never send a hostile message.
- Find out about the other members of the group.
- Accept your share of responsibility for the task.
- Do not let the other participants down by missing a deadline or not fulfilling your share of the tasks without explanation.
- Keep everyone informed of your progress.
- Ask for help if you need it.
- Explore the proposed concepts and ideas.
- Encourage team spirit.

There are probably many other issues, but it should be clear that co-operating requires more than simply fulfilling a task. It is also about developing the members of a group. One benefit that is especially important in the context of this book is that it should help extend everyone's e-learning skills.

Co-operative and collaborative learning methods have been used extensively in traditional courses. In e-learning, many of the ideas have

Activity   Co-operative behaviour

Consider the statements above and how you would implement them. Write down some principles that would help you to participate successfully in a co-operative learning group.

Discussion

There are many different ways of achieving successful co-operation; some of the main are:

1. It is easy to send an email message, so there is a real danger of over- reacting to what seems to be a provocation. A good principle is never to send a critical message without sleeping on it. You will more often regret sending an email than you will not sending one. Reflect on your peer's ideas and views. It is rare than a viewpoint is completely without merit.
2. Don't dismiss any idea without reflecting carefully on it. Just because an idea is from a different perspective, does not mean it is poor. Your perspective may be the incorrect one.
3. Don't monopolise the discussion by sending too many emails. It is important to allow everyone a chance to speak. e-Learning gives considerable freedom to choose when you take part, so some of your peers may be combining studying with a full-time job or family responsibilities which makes it difficult to answer messages immediately.
4. Always ask for feedback from your peers. This may help them participate it they are reluctant.
5. Mailgroups allow you to send an email to all members of the group with a single posting, but you are also free to send an email directly to one member. This is quite useful if you are seeking help or additional information from another member of the group.

What principles did you identify?

been adopted, extended and adapted to fit within the new environment. Co-operative learning can simply be two learners working together, which in a conventional setting probably means sitting next to each other and sharing ideas and comments. It is immediate, whereas a similar e-learning pairing may depend on email – it is asynchronous and is likely to be spread over a longer time.

Some suggestions for launching a co-operative e-learning group are:

- Spend time introducing yourselves – it is important that you understand each other as much as possible. When you are working at a distance the possibilities for misunderstandings are great, so minimise them.

- e-Learning gives everyone more freedom to choose when and where and at what pace to take part, so it is useful to start with the agreement of working methods that are as inclusive as possible.
- Agree on how to undertake the task and what each member would like to personally achieve. This may involve dividing the work into sub-tasks or asking someone to act as the secretary or leader of the group. Be willing to take on responsibilities.
- Be realistic about time – it will almost certainly take longer than you think. Consider the deadline (if you have one) and work backwards so that it is achieved. Consider how long each step will take. Sometimes this planning shows that you are already behind, so you need to change your plans.

Example: Working backwards

Deadline	Final Report – 11th August
Writing report	Four weeks – must begin by 14th July
Evidence location and analysis	Six weeks – must begin by 2 June
Today's date	1st June

Analysis shows you that you must start at once, or reduce the time for some tasks

e-learning co-operative methods

There are many learning approaches and methods used in group and co-operative learning, a number of which are relevant to both traditional and e-learning (Table 8.2). The ones used in e-learning have been adapted to suit the e-learning environment (e.g. learners communicating through email rather than face-to-face). Although email is normally asynchronous, it is possible to mimic a synchronous conversation by asking everyone to take part at a set time. In this way, it is possible for a live event to take place. In some cases, a telephone conference can be operated in parallel. If you are taking part in a synchronous event, it is good practice to have a notebook ready to record your thoughts so you are ready when your opportunity comes to contribute.

Activity 91   Co-operative methods

From your own experience, select one of the above approaches and consider it from a co-operative learning perspective. How would you ensure that the extra dimension of personal development is included in the experience?

Discussion

I selected the competitions/role play approach because it is an approach I normally avoid but one which perhaps I need to understand better. I would:

1. Take on roles that were more demanding than I normally do so that I was able to experience more.
2. Keep a personal diary of the whole activity so I could reflect on what had happened and try to improve my contribution.
3. I would ask someone in the group to give me feedback on my contribution.

You may have decided on quite different methods and actions.

Activity   Co-operative methods – supporting other people

Assisting other learners can be a useful way to help your own learning and an important part of co-operative learning. From your own experience, select one of the above approaches (a different one from the previous activity) and consider it from a co-operative learning perspective. How would you ensure that you support your peers?

Discussion

I selected the debates/discussion circles, since it is an interesting method and I have taken part in a wide variety of them.

1. I would try express my own ideas in a straightforward way.
2. I would always try to be polite and constructive in all my comments.
3. I would be willing to give feedback if requested.
4. I would encourage participation.
5. I would consider carefully all messages and be willing to admit that more relevant ideas than my own had been suggested.

These all sound a little self-righteous but the key point is to respect your peers and be open to new concepts.

Table 8.2   e-Learning co-operative methods

Method	Comments
Brainstorm	Brainstorming sessions are intended to have a large degree of spontaneity with individual contributions sparking ideas from other participants. The initial round of thoughts is usually not assessed, the subject or issue being thoroughly explored before you start to consider practical issues.
	An e-learning equivalent tries to achieve the same results but is likely to last a few days rather than the few hours that a face-to-face event would require. It needs a moderator to maintain time limits and to gather all the ideas together so assessment can be systematically undertaken.
Buzz groups	Buzz groups are often used in the classroom or conference hall to generate questions or to quickly discuss the speakers' ideas. They normally last only a few minutes and are informal, with a small group of participants (i.e. 3 or 4 people) being asked to discuss a concept quickly. One member is asked to feedback comments.
	They are used for similar purposes in synchronous e-learning (e.g. video and audio conferencing). In asynchronous groups it is difficult to achieve the speed and natural conversation so they are rarely used.
Competitions/ role play	Competitions that allow individuals to explore complex situations are an effective way of motivating groups and individuals. Different groups are asked to compete with each other. This can take the form of each group member role-playing a particular situation (e.g. each group acting as a business in competition with others for a contract).
	Online competitions are very effective and can involve consideration of complex and involved situations. A face-to-face role-play competition may only last a few hours, while an e-learning one may need several weeks. However, the longer period allows for detailed analysis of information to decide on decisions, so providing more opportunities for in-depth study.
Informal discussion	Learning often takes place in informal settings away from the classroom or laboratory, e.g., in the corridor after a lecture, over a cup of coffee or walking between locations. Anywhere that learners can meet and talk is a potential place for learning.
	In e-learning you are often separated from other learners so that virtual informal locations need to be created, such as cybercafes where you can discuss the course or anything else with your peers.
Debates/ Discussion Circles	Face-to-face debates and discussions are a useful means of exploring issues. Often the topic is polarised into two opposing views in order to test its extremes.
	In e-learning a paper is often presented to provide a foundation for the debate or discussion. Participants are allowed to contribute their

→

Table 8.2   e-Learning co-operative methods – *continued*

Method	Comments
	views on the paper – extending its argument or criticising it. Often a series of parallel discussions on different issues forms.
	The debates can last many weeks or a few days and are moderated to ensure that they remain focused. Often at the end, a summary of the discussion is provided.
Interviews	Conventional interviews allow the views of an expert to be presented to an audience and offer the opportunity for audience members to ask supplementary questions, although in practice in a large group few will be able to speak.
	An expert and interviewer undertake a normal question and answer session, the difference being that it is sent to the whole group as a series of emails. The group can join in by commenting on the answers and asking supplementary questions.
Investigations	In small groups, you are asked to carry out an investigation of a particular topic. Normally you will be provided with a starting point (e.g. a document or website) but you have to decide how to proceed and to produce a report of your results. The main difference between traditional and e-learning investigations is immediacy. e-learning investigations last longer.
Pairs	Two learners helping each other to learn will share views, assist with problems, review material and discuss the course content. It may be a formal or informal arrangement in that the learners themselves have decided to study together. Again, the main differences are distance and time.
Panels	Panels of experts are often used in seminars and conferences to facilitate the scrutiny of a subject. In a similar way, e-panels allow you to question a group of specialists in order to reveal the issues.
Projects	e-Projects are very similar to face-to-face ones, the significant difference being that you do not meet your partners. You need to decide on a division of the tasks, time scales and the form of reporting back to the group. Groupware applications can help project teams to co-operate.
Quests	A special form of online investigation but normally you are provided with a list of websites so that you are not searching for information but analysing it. In some cases each member of the group is given a role to play during the quest.
Stories	A creative use of online communication is to write a story jointly with a number of colleagues. An initial paragraph is provided and everyone is allowed to add the next paragraph of the story.
	This can be an interesting and fun experience.

Activity   Online learning group and co-operative skills assessment

Table 8.3 provides a structure for you to assess your current level of skill, what future level you would like to achieve and what opportunities you aim to take in order to develop your skills.

Table 8.3   Online learning group and co-operative skills assessment

Skill	Current skill level	Opportunities to develop skill
Using communication technology		
Interpersonal skills		
Group formation		
Co-operation		

Discussion

The example in Table 8.4 is intended to show some possible areas you may wish to consider.

Table 8.4   Personalised online learning group and co-operative skills assessment

Skill	Current skill level	Opportunities to develop skill
Using communication technology	Experienced user of email. Occasional participant in video and audio conferencing. Rarely use chat.	Join a chatroom discussing a topic that interests me to develop a more informal synchronous communication style.

➜

▶ Online seminars and conferences

There is a role for more large-scale e-learning events such as an online seminar or conference. Table 8.5 compares a traditional conference

Activity   Online learning group and co-operative skills assessment – *continued*

Table 8.4   Personalised online learning group and co-operative skills assessment – *continued*

Skill	Current skill level	Opportunities to develop skill
Interpersonal skills	Good face-to-face skills, but have less experience of working with others through communication technology.	I will seek to join a voluntary self-help group that some of my fellow students are establishing. I will attempt to transfer my face-to-face skills to the new environment.
Group formation	Experienced participant in face-to-face groups, but rarely feel comfortable as the leader. Occasionally joined online groups but rarely contribute.	Need to be more than a lurker. I should volunteer to take responsibility for a task and make an effort to fully participate. I will keep a record of my contributions and monitor myself.
Co-operation	Reliable member of a group but only occasionally have I reached out to help others take part or considered if I or the others have grown through the experience.	The course includes completion of a group project. I will use this as an opportunity to see if I can actively co-operate with other students. I will reflect on what happens and seek to identify how I can improve my skills.

What did you identify?

with an online or virtual confeence. At traditional conferences you are limited to a single theme at any one time, but online conferences allow you to take part in many different themes while continuing with your normal work or studies, since you are working asynchronously.

Table 8.5 Comparing traditional and online conferences

Conference feature	Traditional	Online
Keynote speaker	Everyone assembles and listens to an expert	An expert produces a paper and/or PowerPoint presentation which is sent to everyone enrolled in the conference Alternatively the paper and/or presentation are available to be downloaded from a conference website
Parallel themes	A series of rooms are prepared and individual speakers present their work and answer questions	A series of mailgroups are established for each theme and the paper is sent to each registered delegate. They are then free to ask questions of the speaker
Workshops	A series of rooms is prepared and facilitators attempt to focus participants on addressing the issues of the workshop	A series of mailgroups are established for each workshop and the facilitator acts as the moderator of the group
Posters	An area is set aside and each participant is given a space to illustrate their work. This normally consists of a wall poster display and supporting papers	Each poster is shown on a webpage with email connection to the participants so their work can be discussed

➜

If you consider the comparisons in Table 8.5 you will see that an online event offers advantages over a conventional conference such as:

- you can participate in almost everything;
- you can combine the event with your normal activities;
- there are no travel and subsistence costs.

However, the conference takes place over a long period and, in order to gain the maximum benefit from the event, it does require you to organise yourself. It is good practice to:

Table 8.5 Comparing traditional and online conferences – *continued*

Conference feature	Traditional	Online
	At designated times the participants are available to discuss their work with conference delegates.	
Exhibition	An area is provided in which stands showing the products from the different exhibitors are set up.	Exhibitors provide links to their own websites with email connection so delegates can make enquiries
	Delegates are able to walk around, look at each stand and discuss the products with company representatives.	
Informal discussion	An important aspect of any conference is the chance meetings with people who share similar interests	Informal contact is often provided through a conference chatroom
Time	Traditional conferences are time limited. They range from one day to a week	Online conferences often last several weeks since delegates are often involved part-time while carrying on with a full-time job or course

- plan to take part regularly (e.g. every evening) – it is difficult to catch up if you fall behind with the debate;
- keep records of issues and ideas so you can reflect on them later;
- avoid over-extendeding yourself by trying to take part in too many parallel discussions – it is easy to deceive yourself that you can cope with multiple themes only to find yourself falling behind in them all; it is better practice to focus on what interests you most;
- contact individual participants directly if they raise issues that you are especially interested in – this is the equivalent of talking to presenters at the end of their session or introducing yourself to another conference delegate so you can discuss their work.

Activity   Peer assessment

Consider one or two of your student colleagues and attempt to assess their contribution to a group exercise that you have participated in with them.

Discussion

The initial issue when you are assessing peers is to be objective and not simply respond to their personalities and your own feelings. Consider:

1. the aims and objectives of the group activity;
2. what the group agreed to do – roles that were allocated, any timetable for action.

Write down what you feel the people you are assessing contributed in this context. Did they achieve what they agreed to do? Did they contribute more than their fair share? Did they cause other group members problems (e.g. by being late with their work)? Did they solve other group members problems?
    Compare your own contribution with your peers since this will help with the objectivity of your assessment. Try to assess your peers as you would like to be assessed in turn.

▶ Peer assessment

A feature of many group, collaborative or co-operative activities is that your contribution is assessed by your peers as well as your tutors. You will, of course, be asked to assess your colleagues. The assessment can take many forms but it does place a responsibility on you to make objective judgements. You may also be asked to judge your own performance.

It is useful during the group work to consider:

*   Your own performance – how would you improve your contribution – why is it helpful?
*   Who made the most valuable contribution and why?
*   Who made the least contribution and why?

The key issue is to be objective and fair in your assessment.

▶ Summary

1. **Group working online**
    Although e-learning often involves individual learning groups,

collaborative learning also plays a major role. Group activities encourage you to compare yourself with other learners, provides peer support and motivation to develop new skills. Although there are many similarities between face-to-face and e-learning groups, a significant difference is often immediacy. Email exchanges can be spread over days, with delays, reflecting the different members' behaviour in using the technology.

Group formation
Groups of all types take time to form. They require active participants, which can sometimes mean that disagreement is part of the formation process. e-Learning groups will often take longer to form than their face-to-face equivalents.

Comparing face-to-face with e-learning groups
There are both similarities and differences between face-to-face and e-learning groups. Some of the main differences are related to:

- **Time** – e-learning groups will normally need more time to complete a task.
- **Delays** – responses from participants and tutors will always experience a time delay due to using email.
- **Writing** – normally e-learning groups will communicate in writing.
- **Multiple topics** – e-learning groups can discuss several topics in parallel.
- **Participants** – e-learning groups can be larger than face-to-face groups and can co-operate with other groups.
- **Equality** – email allows everyone to participate, but many people choose to take a passive role.
- **Records** – a full record of all email discussions can automatically be kept.

2. **Co-operative learning**
Co-operative learning is about a group of learners working together. It is not limited to undertaking a task, but is concerned with developing participants (e.g. improving individual learning skills). Some suggestions for launching a co-operative e-learning group are:

- spend time introducing yourselves;

- agree work methods that are inclusive;
- agree how to undertake the task and what each member would like to achieve;
- be realistic about time.

e-Learning co-operative methods

There are many learning approaches and methods used in group and co-operative learning, both in traditional and e-learning. Those used in e-learning have been adapted to suit the e-learning environment (e.g. learners communicating through email rather than face-to-face). Methods include brainstorming, buzz groups, competitions/role plays, informal settings, debates/discussion circles, interviews, investigations, pairs, panels, projects, quests and stories.

3. **Online seminars and conferences**

    There is a role for more large scale e-learning events such as an online seminar or conference with a variety of ways of organising these. Some potential advantages of online events are:

    - you can participate in almost everything;
    - you can combine the event with your normal activities;
    - no travel and subsistence costs are incurred.

    However, the conference can take place over several weeks or months and gaining maximum benefit from the event does require self-organisation.

4. **Peer assessment**

    In group activities your contribution may be assessed by your peers. This can take a variety of forms, including also assessing your own performance.

9 Further Information and Resources

A wide range of additional information and resources is provided here, with annotations. This will assist the reader to further develop their skills and understanding of e-learning. Websites are dynamic and although all these sites were running at the time of going to print, some are likely to change.

Acceptable use policies
www.becta.org.uk – British Educational Communication Technology Agency provides support and assistance to education in the United Kingdom. The website contains many useful resources including acceptable use policies

Adult learning
www.waytolearn.co.uk/ – information about adult learning opportunities in England

www.careers-scotland.org.uk/ – information about adult learning in Scotland

www.bbc.co.uk/ – BBC Online provides access to online learning resources

www.beskilled.net/ – information about adult learning in Wales

www.niace.org.uk – National Institute for Adult Continuing Education in England and Wales

Assessing quality of online resources
www.sosig.ac.uk/desire/internet-detective.html – interactive tutorial

Biography
www.biography.com/ – many thousands of biographies

www.s9.com/biography/ – biographical dictionary

http://amillionlives.com/ – links to many biographical resources

www.anb.org/ – American National Biography

Books
www.abebooks.co.uk – worldwide used and out of print books

www.amazon.com – probably the best-known online bookshop in the world

www.bookbrain.co.uk – this search engine will help you to locate a book in a range of online bookshops. It compares prices and the cost of postage and packing

www.booksinprint.com/ – how to locate any book which is currently available

www.thebookplace.co.uk/ – The Book Pl@ce

Buying a computer
www.oft.gov.uk/ – United Kingdom's Office for Fair Trading have published a leaflet on buying computers for consumers. It is available from their website.

Chat
http://chat.yahoo.com/ – Yahoo Chat rooms

Databases
www.bl.uk/ – British Library

www.eric.ed.gov/ – Educational Resource Information Centre – major educational resource; databases, journals and publications

www.music.indiana.edu/ – lists of music databases

http://libraries.maine.edu/mariner – list of many research databases

www.lib.duke.edu/ – list of research databases compiled by Duke University

www.lib.washington.edu/ – top 20 research databases compiled by the Washington University

www.profusion.com – lists of databases that allow you to search for the subject or topic of your choice

Dictionaries
http://dictionary.reference.com/ – online dictionary

www.askoxford.com/ – online dictionary

www.oed.com/ – Oxford English Dictionary, subscription service

Disabilities
www.abilityhub.com/ – Abilityhub, information about assistive technology

www.abilitynet.org.uk – Abilitynet, a charity which provides help, advice and support in using ICT for disabled people

www.abledata.com/ – Abledata, information about assistive technology

www.cast.org/bobby – Bobby is an accessibility standard for web pages; it will assess your pages to check if they conform with the accessibility standard for disabled users

www.closingthegap.com/ – Closing The Gap Inc, an organisation that provides help with technology for people with special needs, 526 Main Street, PO Box 68, Henderson, Minnesota 56044, USA

www.drc-gb.org/ – Disability Rights Commission

www.dyslexic.com/ – help with dyslexia

www.rnib.org.uk – Royal National Institute of the Blind (RNIB)

www.rnid.org.uk – Royal National Institute of the Deaf (RNID)

www.techdis.ac.uk/ – help for disabled students and staff in high and further education

www.trace.wisc.edu – The Trace Research and Development Center (University of Wisconsin-Madison) concentrates on making ICT more available and useful to disabled people

www.youreable.com – Youreable, an organisation to provide information for disabled people

Document format
www.adobe.com – Portable document format creation and reading

www.microsoft.com/ – Electronic document/book creation and reading software

Email addresses
http://people.yahoo.com – large list of individual addresses

Educational resources
www.aace.org/ – Association for the Advancement of Computing in Education

www.aclearn.net – resources for adult learning

www.alt.ac.uk/ – Association for Learning Technology

www.ed.gov/free/ – USA Federal Government Educational Resources

www.educationindex.com/education_resources.html – lists of educational sites on the internet

http://ferl.becta.org.uk/ – Further Education Resources for Learning website

www.csu.edu.au/education/library.html – Education Virtual Library

www.ltscotland.com/ – Learning and Teaching Scotland

www.moneymatterstome.co.uk – online resources for financial capability

www.rdn.ac.uk – resource discovery network; sources of reviewed web resources

Emoticons
Definition of a wide range of emoticons:

www.computeruser.com/resources/dictionary/emoticons.html

www.cknow.com/ckinfo/emoticons.htm

English
www.bbc.co.uk/worldservice/learningenglish/ – help with learning English Language

E-portfolio
www.educause.edu/ – National Learning Infrastructure Initiative
http://www.nottingham.ac.uk/ – Nottingham University examples of e-portfolios

Glossary

www.cnet.com/Resources/Info/Glossary/ – internet terms glossary

www.sharpened.net/glossary/index.php – computer and internet terms glossary

Health and safety

http://europe.osha.eu.int/ – European agency for safety and health at work

www.hhs.gov/ – USA Department of Health and Human Services

www.hse.gov.uk/ – UK Health and Safety Executive

ICT

www.e-skills.com – sector skills council for ICT user skills

www.learndirect.co.uk – learndirect, provider of many e-learning courses

Information

http://europa.eu.int/ – European Union

www.nhsdirect.nhs.uk/ – National Health Service

www.number-10.gov.uk – the Office of the British Prime Minister, 10 Downing Street

www.ukonline.gov.uk/ – information for the British Citizen

www.un.org/ – United Nations

www.vts.rdn.ac.uk/ – virtual training suite, free tutorials to develop your information skills

www.whitehouse.gov/ – USA President's White House

Internet resources

www.bbc.co.uk/learning/ – BBC television learning resources

www.clearinghouse.net – this is a list of internet resource guides, but unfortunately is no longer actively maintained

www.channel4.com/ – Channel Four Television offers learning materials

www.rdn.ac.uk – Resource Discovery Network assessed web resources

www.vlib.org.uk – essential catalogue of internet resources

Journals
Many journals are only available on subscription. Your college or employer may be able to provide you with access to them.

www.lib.washington.edu/types/ejournals/ – a list of electronic journals compiled by the University of Washington

http://olt-bta.hrdc-drhc.gc.ca/resources/ejournalsx.html – Canadian Office for Learning Technology list of e-journals relating to learning technologies

http://scholar.lib.vt.edu/ejournals/JTE/ – Journal of Technology Education.

www.scre.ac.uk/is/webjournals.html – SCRE Centre, University of Glasgow list of e-journals.

www.usdla.org/html/journal/ – Journal of the US Distance Learning Association.

Learning centres (ICT)
http://cybercaptive.com/ – this is a search engine to help you locate a cybercafe near to you

www.dfes.gov.uk/ukonlinecentres/ – UK Online Centres are a government initiative to provide public access to information and communication technology.

www.helpisathand.gov.uk/ – Help is at Hand is a website to support the staff of UK online centres.

www.learndirect.co.uk/ – Learndirect organise a network of centres in the UK providing access to a wide range of online training courses, including many related to developing ICT skills

www.peoplesnetwork.gov.uk/ – People's Network is a government initiative to provide ICT facilities at all public libraries in Great Britain

Learning styles
www.ncsu.edu/felder-public/ILSdir/ilsweb.html – Learning Style Questionnaires

Libraries
http://bl.uk/catalogues/blpc.html – the British Library public catalogue

www.lii.org – Librarian's Index to the Internet

www.ipl.org/ – Internet Public Library

www.loc.gov/ – the Library of Congress, search the catalogue

www.loc.gov/global/library/library.html – Library of Congress internet resources

www.ifla.org/International Federation of Library Associations and Institutions

www.nla.gov.au – National Library of Australia

www.nlb-online.org/ – National Library for the Blind

http://portico.bl.uk/gabriel/index.html – European National Libraries

www.questia.com/ – Online Library

Mailgroups
www.jiscmail.ac.uk – list of mailgroups for Higher and Further Education in Great Britain provided by Joint Information Systems Committee

www.lsoft.com/lists/listref.html – list of listserv mailgroups

Managed Learning Environments
www.jisc.ac.uk/mle/ – Joint Information Systems Committee is a United Kingdom educational advisory body that provides help on the use of technology in learning.

http://ferl.becta.org.uk/ – FERL site operated by the British Educational Communication Technology Agency contains information about Managed and Virtual Learning Environments

Netiquette
www.albion.com/netiquette/corerules.html

www.fau.edu/netiquette/net/

www.learnthenet.com/english/html/09netiqt.htm

Plagiarism
www.mydropbox.com/ – site aimed at stopping plagiarism in higher education

http://online.northumbria.ac.uk/faculties/art/information_studies/I mri/Jiscpas/site/jiscpas.asp – plagiarism advisory service

Quality
www.sosig.ac.uk/desire/internet-detective.html – online tutorial on evaluating web-based content

Search engines

AltaVista	http://altavista.com/
	www.uk.altavista.com/
AllThe Web.com	www.alltheweb.com
Ask Jeeves	www.askjeeves.com
Dogpile	www.dogpile.com/
Excite	www.excite.com/
Google	www.google.co.uk
HotBot	www.hotbot.com/
Looksmart	www.looksmart.com/
Lycos	www-uk.lycos.com/
MSN Search	http://search.msn.com
Metacrawler	www.metacrawler.com
Northern Lights	www.nlsearch.com/
Webcrawler	www.webcrawler.com/
Yahoo	www.yahoo.co.uk

Shareware
www.shareware.com – search for shareware

Study
www.mantex.co.uk/homepage.htm – books, reviews and other help with studying

www.skills4study.com – information, help and guidance on studying effectively, whatever your level, discipline or need

Tools
www.winzip.com/ – compression tool

Virtual experiments
www.chem.ox.ac.uk/vrchemistry/labintro/newdefault.html – University of Oxford examples of virtual experiments in chemistry

www.explorescience.com/ – scientific experiments for children www.online-edu.com/products/pintar_pro.htm – tools for developing virtual experiments

Virtual Learning Environments
See Managed Learning Environments

Yellow Pages
www.wayp.com/ – this is a site which provides access to international addresses and telephone numbers

WebQuest
http://webquest.sdsu.edu/overview.htm – San Diego State University WebQuest Resources

Appendix A: Assessing your learning skills

e-Learning requires a mixture of many different skills. Some of them should be familiar to you from other learning experiences, but many have been changed or modified to fit within the online environment. Table A.1 contains many of the key skills for e-learning. At the start of studying this book it is worthwhile assessing your current skills and then, as you undertake the various activities within the book, return to the assessment and consider your progress.

The list below is cross referenced to the different parts of the book, providing you with a study map if you are seeking to improve a particular aspect of your skills. Appendix C provides a checklist of your ICT skills.

Table A.1   Assessing e-learning skills

e-Learning skills	Comments	Suggestions for improvement	Assessment
Reading	Browsing or being able to scan a text for the key points is an important skill when reading online content	Chapter 2 traditional Learning skills Chapter 4 e-journals, online databases and libraries Chapter 7 online communication	
Writing	1. Keyboard – this is one of the main ways of communicating through a computer, so it is a core skill		

Table A.1 Assessing e-learning skills – *continued*

e-Learning skills	Comments	Suggestions for improvement	Assessment
	2. Assignments – this is essentially the same skill that you need for traditional studies 3. Notes – taking notes is essential in many forms of learning 4. email and other communication messages – this is the skill of being able to write concise but clear messages that convey your ideas, views and concerns	Chapter 2 traditional learning skills Chapter 4 communication technology and learning environments Chapter 7 online communication	
Collaborate and co-operate with other learners	Many forms of e-learning require you to collaborate or co-operate with other learners	Chapter 8 collaborative and co-operative learning	
Reflection	Learning through your experiences is a part of all forms of learning	Chapter 5 e-learning reflection Chapter 6 more practice	
Time management	Being able to manage your studies is particularly important if you are an e-learning student since you are relying on yourself	Chapter 5 e-learning time management Chapter 6 more practice	
Acceptance of responsibility	When you are an e-learner you are mainly responsible for your own learning. In many cases no one else will remind you about deadlines, etc.	Chapter 2 traditional learning skills Chapter 5 e-learning acceptance of responsibility	

Table A.1   Assessing e-learning skills – *continued*

e-Learning skills	Comments	Suggestions for improvement	Assessment
Planning	e-Learners often need to be able to efficiently plan their studies so they fit into their wider responsibilities	Chapter 5 e-learning planning Chapter 6 more practice	
Searching skills – world wide web	This is a complex set of knowledge and skills involving the understanding of different types of search engines and search techniques (e.g. Boolean)	Chapter 3 searching the web	
Navigation	To move around the world wide web's structure you need to understand hypertext links and the navigation features of browsers	Many of the activities within the book require you to practise your navigation skills	
Assessing quality – world wide web	Locating sites is one important skill, but being able to judge the quality of the information is another related skill	Chapter 3 judging the quality of websites Many activities throughout the book require you to judge quality of online content	
Self-assessment	This involves a combination of skills such as considering feedback, asking questions and being well-informed about required standards	Chapter 5 e-learning self-assessment Chapter 6 more practice	
Peer-assessment	In some e-learning courses learners are asked to assess each others' contributions	Chapter 8 peer assessment	

Table A.1   Assessing e-learning skills – *continued*

e-Learning skills	Comments	Suggestions for improvement	Assessment
Problem solving	1. Individually 2. Within a group	Chapter 5 e-learning problem solving Chapter 6 more practice	
Coping with stress	All forms of learning can be stressful but studying on your own is often particularly prone to stress	Chapter 2 traditional learning skills Chapter 5 e-learning and coping with stress Chapter 6 more practice	
Motivating yourself	Motivation is key to successful learning, so being able to motivate yourself is particularly important	Chapter 5 e-learning motivation Chapter 6 more practice	
Research	Investigating a topic is part of many forms of learning	Chapter 2 traditional learning skills Chapter 3 searching the web and judging the quality of websites Chapter 4 e-journals, online databases and libraries Chapter 5 e-learning research skills Chapter 6 more practice	

Appendix B: Tips for the successful e-learning student

1. **Collaborate** – the online environment provides you with many opportunities to co-operate with your peers, to share and reflect on your experience of e-learning. If you participate fully in the experience, you will benefit both through your personal experience and also from your peers.

2. **Writing skills** are the key to online communication. You need to be able to write short clear messages to communicate your needs, ideas and views by email. However, remember netiquette so that you are not offensive.

3. **Reading skills** are important in that a large amount of the e-learning content is written.

4. **Motivation** – you are in control of when, where and at what pace you learn, but you must be able to motivate yourself to take advantage of the opportunities that this flexibility provides

5. **Confidence** – e-learning provides you with many opportunities but you must have the confidence to take advantage of them (e.g. to take the initiative and contact your peers).

6. **Commitment** – the freedom to choose when you learn must be accompanied by a regular commitment to the course. It is better in most cases to give a small regular commitment of time to the course than an occasional large effort.

7. **Use your tutor** – e-learning can often feel lonely and isolating, but you have a tutor so use him or her. When you have a ques-

tion, doubt or simply want to check something, contact your tutor. Tutors are there to help you.

8. **Miscellaneous** – there are many small tips that will make your more successful. They include:

   - check your email regularly (e.g. daily);
   - allow people time to respond to your messages and remember that everyone else has the same freedom to learn when they want to;
   - tell everyone if your email address changes;
   - keep a record of you passwords and User ID in a safe place;
   - backup your records regularly.

9. **Manage your time** – you need to plan your studying and assignments. It is important to be realistic about how much you can achieve in a given time period.

10. **Manage your own environment** – it is important to organise yourself to make your environment suitable for learning. This includes:

    - taking regular breaks;
    - giving yourself time for reflection;
    - creating space for your books, files and computer – everything should be close to you when you are studying so your concentration is not broken.

11. **Explore/investigate** – the online environment has been designed to help you learn. It is useful to explore this new world to understand how best it can help you with your studies.

12. **Feedback** – there are many opportunities to receive feedback from peers and tutors, so take advantage of them by carefully considering all they offer.

13. **Computer skills** – it is vital to start your e-learning with a basic foundation of computer skills, but you will need to develop these by using every problem as an opportunity to learn new skills.

14. **Employ the resources provided** – e-learning courses offer

many different resources for you so make sure you are aware of them, for example:

- online conferences;
- chatrooms;
- interactive learning materials;
- self-assessment tests.

15. **Learning style** – it is useful to be aware of your own learning preferences so that you can make informed decisions about the course.

Appendix C: Assessing your ICT skills

In order to be a successful e-learner you must have good ICT skills. Chapter 3 provides an introduction to some aspects of the knowledge and skills you will need, but this checklist provides a more comprehensive means of assessing your competence. If you need to develop your technical skills, many colleges provide short courses for students or, if you are studying in the United Kingdom, learndirect offers many ICT e-learning courses (www.learndirect.co.uk) or visit the e-skills website for information about ICT user skills (www.e-skills.com).

Table C.1 Assessing ICT skills

Task	Sub-task	Assessment
Switch equipment on and off		
Open applications (e.g. word-processing, spreadsheets and databases)		
Close applications		
Use Microsoft Windows operating system	1. Resize windows 2. Select icons 3. Choose menus options 4. Use scroll bars 5. Use toolbars 6. Use Help	
Adjust Microsoft Windows Accessibility options	1. Changing the contrast 2. StickyKeys 3. FilterKeys 4. ToggleKeys 5. SoundSentry 6. ShowSounds 7. Cursor blink rates and width	

Table C.1   Assessing ICT skills – *continued*

Task	Sub-task	Assessment
	8. Controlling the mouse pointer with the keyboard number pad	
Use a keyboard	1. Enter text and numbers 2. Special function keys (e.g. insert, ctrl and alt) 3. Function keys 4. Num and Caps lock	
Use a mouse	1. Click left and right buttons 2. Drag and drop 3. Highlight	
Save and transport information	1. Onto floppy disks 2. Onto USB memory sticks (dongles) 3. CD-Read Write disks	
Use a digital camera	1. Take pictures 2. Store on computer	
Use a scanner	1. Pictures 2. Text	
Word-processing	1. Enter 2. Insert text 3. Insert pictures 4. Insert tables 5. Delete 6. Copy 7. Cut 8. Paste 9. Drag and drop 10. Find and replace 11. Undo and redo 12. Save 13. Save as 14. Print 15. Track changes	
Spreadsheets	1. Enter 2. Insert text 3. Delete 4. Copy	

Table C.1 Assessing ICT skills – *continued*

Task	Sub-task	Assessment
	5. Cut	
	6. Paste	
	7. Drag and drop	
	8. Find and replace	
	9. Undo and redo	
	10. Save	
	11. Save as	
	12. Print	
	13. Formula	
	14. Charts and Graphs	
Databases	1. Search for information	
	2. Add information to a database	
	3. Print information	
Manage files and folders	1. Open	
	2. Close	
	3. Save	
	4. Save as	
	5. Print	
	6. Rename	
	7. Identify different formats	
	8. Compress files	
	9. Create folders	
Use the internet	1. Connect to internet	
	2. Enter website addresses (URLs)	
	3. Navigate websites	
	4. Use search engines • use directories • use meta-engines • use multiple search criteria • relational operators e.g. =, >, <=, logical operators AND and OR	
	5. Navigate websites • hyperlinks • forward and back • save and use favourites	
Use email	1. Open email application	
	2. Open emails inbox	

Table C.1   Assessing ICT skills – *continued*

Task	Sub-task	Assessment
	3. Use emails • delete • produce new messages • send • forward • insert attachments • use an address book • employ netiquette • use distribution lists	
Viruses	Configure virus protection software to protect your system	

Appendix D: Main sources of dissatisfaction

Hara and Koling (2000) have identified two major sources of frustration for e-learners. They are:

1. **Technical** – all forms of technical problems can be a nuisance and severely distract you from your studies. There are several ways of dealing with them:

- College helpdesk – your college may provide a student help line to assist you with software and hardware problems. However, in some cases this is limited to the software and hardware they have supplied with the course.
- Warranty – your equipment may be covered by a warranty from the suppliers that will often include a telephone help line, although sometimes you have to pay extra for the call. In addition, an engineer may call if the problem is too difficult to resolve over the telephone or they may collect your equipment to repair at their centre. You need to study warranties. Ideally you need one which guarantees how long they will take to come out and repair your equipment. Many simply offer to take away and repair the equipment with no time limit. The initial step is almost always a telephone diagnostic process to identify the problem.
- Applications – many technical problems arise from applications. Many major application suppliers provide websites with technical advice and some (Microsoft) build troubleshooting features into their products.

2. **Teaching**
- Many e-learning programmes will provide you with a personal tutor, mentor or learning supporter. They are first place to go to seek support and help with teaching and learning problems.
- If you are new to e-learning it is often difficult to judge if the

problem is with the teaching or yourself. The easiest way is to ask
your fellow students. What do they think?
- Your college will almost certainly have a complaints procedure if
the problem is serious. This will often be available on the course
website.

Glossary

Explanation of the technical and specialist terms used in e-learning

Adobe Acrobat a document file format which is widely used on the internet for disseminating publications. The file can be identified by its extension .pdf – portable document format. The files need the Adobe Acrobat reader to open and this is available for free

ADSL Asymmetric Digital Subscriber Line – a high-speed telephone line designed for exchanging electronic data (ADSL is replacing ISDN lines)

Applets small programmes that often provide interactive features on websites and online learning materials

assistive technology adaptive equipment and alternative methods for helping disabled people to use information and computer technology

asynchronous a communication method that does not require the learners or tutors to be online at the same time

authoring the process of creating computer-based learning materials

authoring system software tool or application that assists you to create e-learning materials

back up make a copy of your files to prevent the loss of your work. It applies to simply copying a single electronic document or all your files. There are many ways of backing up your information such as writing the data to a CD-RW or DVD-RW disk.

bandwidth this is the size of the connection you have with the internet. The larger the bandwidth the faster and more effective the service you will be able to get

BBS   Bulletin Board Systems

blended learning   a mix of several different learning approaches (e.g. traditional classrooms methods combined with e-learning)

blogging   a public but personal online diary or journal based on a website

bobby   a webpage accessibility standard for disabled users

bookmark   this is the way that browsers allow you to mark a webpage so that you can quickly locate it again. It is sometimes called a 'favorite'.

browser   this is an application that allows you to view, save and print websites

bulletin board   an online location where you can post and collect messages

button   small area which, if you click on it, will move you to a new area of the package or open a feature

CAI   Computer Assisted Instruction – a name for some forms of e-learning material (see also CAL, CBT and TBT)

CAL   Computer Assisted Learning – a name for some forms of e-learning materials (see also CAI, CBT and TBT)

CBT   Computer-Based Training – a name for some forms of e-learning materials (see also CAI, CAL and TBT)

chat   online synchronous text communication

CGI   Common Gateway Interface

citation   if you have used the contents of a book, journal article or other resource in an essay or other form of work, you must cite the author in your text and give the full reference so that readers can locate your source. This is called a citation.

collaborative learning   learning in and with a group of other learners

compression   a method of making a large file smaller so that it can be more easily transported (see zip)

Computer-based learning   learning material delivered and supported through the use of a computer

Computer Mediated Communication (CMC)   the use of communication technologies to allow people to communicate while living or working at a distance from each other

conferencing   there are many forms of online conference, but essentially it is a platform in which a group of people can meet virtually in a variety of ways. Many conferences will combine mailgroups, bulletin boards and chat rooms

cookies   these are small pieces of information that websites place on your computer to allow them to recognise the patterns of your visits to their site so that they can customise their service to you

courseware   these are chunks of e-learning materials. They can vary in size from a single chunk covering a small piece of learning to an entire learning or training course

dial-up   this is the most straightforward way of connecting to the internet, through a telephone line which is also used for normal calls

download   when you move a file of electronic information (e.g. a picture, acrobat file, etc.) from a website to your own computer the process is called downloading

e-learning   learning which is supported and delivered through the use of information and communication technology

emoticon   the use of small symbols or punctuation marks to convey emotion in e-messages or chat

encryption   to protect information by encoding it (i.e. turning it into code using a special application)

e-portfolio   an electronic collection of evidence to demonstrate your knowledge, understanding and competence in your subject

extranet   a single organisation intranet which has some aspects open to external users, although these are often password protected

FAQ   Frequently Asked Questions – lists of questions which users of websites and other online resources have asked in the past. They are displayed on a website and online resource to help new users

firewall   a security system which protects a computer from unauthorised access

flame   an angry or offensive email message

freeware (open source applications)   free software the use of which is usually unlimited

FTP (File Transfer Protocol)   a method of transferring a file over the internet

GIF   an image file format

GUI   Graphic User Interface

Groupware   applications that allow people linked through a network (e.g. internet) to share information and work co-operatively and collaboratively

help desk   technical support service often accessed by telephone

home page   this is the first page of a website and often serves the purpose of explaining the nature of the website

HTML   Hypertext Markup Language

Hypertext Markup Language   this is the language in which websites are constructed so that a browser can view them

icon   small picture symbol which links you to other areas of a website or system, or opens an application

ILT (Information and Learning Technology)   another way of saying e-learning (ILT is also the Institute for Learning and Teaching)

information and communication technology   the combination of computer and telecommunication technology

Integrated Service Digital Network (ISDN)   a high-speed telephone line designed for the transfer of computer data (ISDN is being replaced by ADSL lines)

Internet Service Provider (ISP)   this is an organisation that will link you to the internet

intranet   an internet that is limited to a single organisation (e.g. a college)

IRC   Internet Relay Chat

ISDN   Integrated Service Digital Network

ISP   Internet Service Provider, an organisation that offers you a connection to the internet (some also offer other services)

JAVA   a popular programming language often associated with websites

JPEG   an image file format

LAN   Local Area Network of computers

LMS (Learning Management System)   essentially an alternative expression for a Managed Learning Environment or Virtual Learning Environment

Learning objects   a distinct piece of e-learning material that you can combine with other objects to form a programme

lurk   to take a passive part in an online discussion group or conference (i.e. receiving the messages without responding to them)

mailgroups   a group of participants linked through email so that by sending a single email to the group address everyone receives the message

metadata   data about the content of the learning material

m-learning   mobile learning or delivering e-learning through portable communication systems such as a mobile telephone, laptop computer, etc.

modem   this is a piece of equipment that allows you to link your computer to the internet

moderator   the person who takes responsibility for mailgroups and other forms of online communication. They facilitate and encourage discussion

MPEG   a video file format

multicasting   email, video, audio or other form of broadcast across the world wide web

multimedia   the presentation of materials using a mixture of media such as video, sound, animation, text and graphics

netiquette   a set of rules, often mutually agreed, that govern the content of emails and how they are used

newsgroup   a service which allows you to access information on a particular topic

offline   using a computer when it is not linked to the internet

online learning   learning that is delivered and supported through the internet

patch   a software package intended to correct a problem with an existing application

PDA (Personal Digital Assistant)   a handheld computer device

plug-ins   these are additional pieces of software that allow your browser to view extra file formats (e.g. multimedia)

point of presence   a local telephone point which your modem calls to make a telecommunication link to the internet

POP   Point of Presence

portal   a special type of website giving access to a wide range of other related sites and online resources

portfolio   see e-portfolio

real time   synchronous, or at the same time, communication when everyone has to be online to take part

screen reader   an application that reads the text displayed on a computer screen out loud so that visually impaired users can access the system

search engine   an application which searches the world wide web to locate webpages that match your search words

shareware applications   applications that you can use in order to evaluate them before you buy

spam   unrequested emails, in some cases advertising products or services; essentially the electronic equivalent of junk mail

streaming   a technique that allows video and audio to be transmitted so that you can begin watching the video or listening to the audio before the whole content has arrived at your computer. It avoids the long delays due to sending large video or audio files

synchronous   a communication method that requires the learners or tutors to use it at the same time

TBT (Technology based Training)   a name for some forms of e-learning materials (see also CAI, CBT and CBL)

TCP/IP   Transmission Control Protocol/Internet Protocol

thread   a series of email messages that are linked to a particular issue, topic or theme

Transmission Control Protocol/Internet Protocol (TCP/IP) – the standards that underpin the internet

Uniform Resource Locator (URL)   this is the address of a web page (e.g. http://www.bbc.co.uk)

Upload   when you move an electronic file from your computer to a website, the process is called uploading

URL   uniform resource locator

USB   Universal Serial Bus, a device to connect peripherals to a computer

virus   a programme designed to secretly replicate itself without the user's permission or knowledge. Often these programmes are designed to harm your system by deleting critical files or data

W3C   organisation which sets standards for the world wide web

weblog   blogging

webmaster   the person who administers a website

WebQuest   an online investigation utilising the information available on the world wide web

WYSIWYG   What You See Is What You Get – this refers to the appearance of a document or image on the screen compared to its printed appearance (i.e. it is identical)

XML (eXtensible Markup Language)   a new development in languages used to develop websites

zip/unzip   a compressed file format which allows you to send large files over the internet

References and Further Reading

Becker, L. (2004), *How to Manage your Distance and Open Learning Course* (Basingstoke: Palgrave Macmillan).

Clarke, A. (1998), *IT Awareness Raising for Adults* (Department of Education and Employment, Sheffield, OL 254).

Clarke, A. (2001a), *Designing Computer-Based Learning Materials*, (Aldershot: Gower).

Clarke, A. (2001b), *Assessing the Quality of Open and Distance Learning Materials* (Leicester: NIACE).

Clarke, A. (2002a), *Online Learning and Social Exclusion* (Leicester: NIACE).

Clarke, A (2002b), *New CLAIT Student Workbook* (Abingdon: Hodder and Stoughton).

Coombes, H. (2001), *Research Using IT* (Basingstoke: Palgrave Macmillan).

Cottrell, S. (2003), *Skills for Success* (Basingstoke: Palgrave Macmillan).

Cottrell, S. (2003), *The Study Skills Handbook*, 2nd edn (Basingstoke: Palgrave Macmillan).

Cox, R., Dineen, F., Mayes, T., McKendree, J. and Stenning, K. (1999) *Vicarious Learning from Educational Dialogue: Proceedings of the Computer Support for Collaborative Learning* (CSCL), 1999 Conference, eds. C. Haodley and J. Roschelle (Palo Alto, CA: Stanford University Press and Lawrence Erlbaum Associates).

Dodge, B. and March, T. (1995), Some thoughts about WebQuests, http://edweb.sdsu.edu/courses/edtec596/about_webquests.html

Hara, N. and Koling, R. (2000), Students' distress in a web-based distance education course, www.slis.indiana.edu/SCI/wp00-01.html

Health and Safety Executive (2000), *Working with VDUs* (Bootle: HSE Books).

Health and Safety Executive (2003), *Aching Arms (or RSI) in Small Businesses* (Bootle: HSE Books).

Honey, P. and Munford, A. (1986), *A Manual of Learning Styles* (Maidenhead: Peter Honey).

Kolb, D. A. (1984), *Experiential Learning: Experience as the Sources of Learning and Development* (Englewood Cliffs, NJ: Prentice Hall).

Nipper, S. (1989), *Third Generation Distance Learning and Computer Conferencing* (London: Mindweave).

Nonnecke, B. and Preece, J. (2001), *Why Lurkers Lurk* (American Conference on Information Systems).

Palloff, R. M. and Pratt, K. (1999), *Building Learning Communities in Cyberspace: Effective Strategies for the Online Classroom* (San Francisco, CA: Jossey-Bass).

Race, P. (1994), *The Open Learning Handbook* (London: Kogan Page).

Terena & Netskills (2002), *Internet Users' Reference* (Harlow: Addison Wesley).

Index